LOST TREASURES

OF EUROPE

427 PHOTOGRAPHS

EDITED BY HENRY LA FARGE

PANTHEON BOOKS

Manufactured in the U.S.A. by American Book–Stratford Press, Inc.
Plates printed by Photogravure and Color Company, New York 1, N.Y.

CONTENTS

	PAGE
Introduction by Ernest T. DeWald	7
Preface by Henry La Farge	10
Acknowledgements	12
Descriptive List of Plates	14

	PLATES
POLAND	1-23
HOLLAND	24-45
BELGIUM	46-59
RUSSIA	60-83
ENGLAND	84-112
ITALY	113-219
FRANCE	220-294
GERMANY	295-419
AUSTRIA	420-423
HUNGARY	424-427

INTRODUCTION

THE SECOND WORLD WAR has passed on into history and has left a dazed and weakened world to take stock once more of the losses sustained during another period of self-immolation.

Throughout history man has had to face the eventual destruction of himself and of the material evidences of his culture either as the result of Time or from the effects of War. As regards his culture, much of this can be and has been transmitted to succeeding generations by the persistence of his memory, by the toughness of his spirit, and by the vitality of his institutions. But the more tangible, visible evidences of his culture and of his creative spirit, such as the arts of architecture, sculpture and painting, those ever-present reminders of the creative genius latent in man, these indeed are and always have been at the mercy either of the disintegrating processes of time or of the sudden ravages of war. Time has in most cases been the more lenient of the two.

We recall the ruthlessness of the armies of antiquity, razing the cities of their enemies in order to wipe out the traces of rival power or glory. The evidence of their fury has been amply laid bare by the spade of the archaeologist. But even then, as the respect for culture grew apace, there are many instances of conquerors acting more leniently and allowing centers of art and culture to survive. The effect on later generations of this survival is evident to anyone paging through the records of history.

On the whole, movable works of art such as sculpture, painting and the minor arts have had a more fortunate history than has architecture. They could either be hidden for safety or might even be carried off as booty. They had greater chances for survival. It is a matter of record, of course, how many masterpieces of Greek sculpture carried off to Italy have been transmitted to us either in the original or through Roman copies. During the wars in modern times it has been equally true that architecture has sustained the greatest damage and losses as the result of military operations. Improved instruments of destruction and bombing from the air have heightened the possibilities for complete annihilation.

A program to safeguard historical monuments and works of art and to record the damage sustained had already been undertaken by Italy, France and Germany during the First World War. These, however, were the concern of Europe, and America had no part in them.

At the outbreak of the Second World War, similar protective measures for art monuments were initiated by the various European countries, but on a larger scale. However with America's entry into the war a new situation arose. The successful termination of the struggle could only be accomplished by an invasion of Europe. The first points of invasion were to be Italy and France. The success of these operations would imply the eventual invasion of Holland, Belgium, Germany and Austria. Greece, too, would have to bear the bitters of a new invasion. American military forces would be predominant in these invasions. Would America therefore also assume her share of the responsibility to safeguard the cultural heritage of those countries through which the armies marched?

No matter what her particular contributions are and have been to the civilization and culture of the modern world, America has her own cultural roots deep in the traditions of Europe.

7

These may seem in our present mechanistic age as a part of a storybook past. But the effects on our modern structure of society of the democratic ideas, the philosophy and art of Greece, the political and legal organizations of Rome, and the civic, religious, and artistic developments in Italy, France and Germany during the Middle Ages and the Renaissance are too patent to need further elaboration. Time and again during the two and a half centuries of our national existence, our political and intellectual leaders as well as our Average American have crossed the seas to make intimate, firsthand contacts with the surviving evidences of past culture and to draw renewed inspiration therefrom. No amount of book knowledge by itself can equal the experience of actual contact or association. Our great cultural institutions also have done their share in keeping before the eyes and minds of the rising generations the importance and value of the heritage passed on to us from Europe.

This heritage, however, was definitely in jeopardy. In the path of the planned invasions lay some of the world's greatest masterpieces erected by the creative human genius. The realization of the impending tragedy crystallized action on the part of those individuals and institutions in America primarily concerned with the transmission to oncoming generations of their heritage from the past. Whatever the difficulties, it seemed imperative that some measures be taken to minimize this inevitable destruction. The creation by the President of the United States of the Roberts Commission, the incorporation into the Armed Forces of Monuments, Fine Arts and Archives Branches and Divisions, and the presence of the officers of these services both with the advancing forces and with the armies of occupation are all the outgrowth of this action. A unique page was written in the military history of the United States. Not only were war-damaged buildings of historic or artistic importance to be given "first aid" by these services, but active measures were to be taken to avoid as much damage and destruction as possible by briefing the task forces, ground and air, as to the importance and location of significant buildings in the zones of operation.

In England a similar action took place. Monuments and Fine Arts and Archives officers were dispatched to North Africa, Sicily and Italy, others began planning for France, the Low Countries and Germany. The MacMillan Committee was formed. The success attending the first large-scale program to save Europe's artistic heritage, which took place in Sicily and Italy, was the result of the amalgamated efforts of British and American officers acting under the aegis of the Allied Commission for Italy, and was an outstanding example of interallied cooperation. It should be borne in mind that part of the program was always to enlist from the start the responsible museum and Fine Arts personnel of the countries in which the programs were put into effect, and that responsibility was passed to this personnel at the earliest possible moment. Even neutral countries came into the picture. During the activities in Germany, offers were received from Sweden to supply lumber materials for first-aid projects.

But destruction there was bound to be, no matter what precautions were taken. It came from various sources, from air bombardments, from demolitions of retiring armies, and from the action of the advancing armies or from battle. It is difficult to state dogmatically that any one single form of action caused the greatest destruction. It is difficult even to state that air raids in general were more obliterating than ground action, except in instances of concentrated fury visited upon Germany. In general, however, where incendiary attacks were made from the air such as those at Rotterdam and Milan, or where armies ground slowly forward with pulverizing effect, as in Normandy, the Rapido River and Cassino areas, the east coast of Italy, the Arno and the Apennines, the devastation was most extensive. And yet the burned-out hulks of buildings, the façades and walls of which are still standing, are nuclei for attempts at reconstruction and can contain much of historical and architectural value for the future, as is the case with the Parthenon, the palace of Theodoric at Ravenna, or the many ruined abbeys of France and England which have survived past wars and devastations. In such guise the present shells of many a Romanesque church in Pisa or of the palaces at Genoa may resume significance for the future.

However, no resuscitating power can ever bring back the frescoes of Mantegna in Padua or those of Melozzo at Forli.

To the world in general, the disappearance of many of its treasures of architecture and art constitutes an irreplaceable loss out of its storehouse of culture and history. No records of human achievement coming to us from the past can be so convincing as those which we can see and touch. And no amount of romantic reconstruction, once the monument is gone, can equal in effectiveness and conviction the original which contained within itself the very essence of its period in history. Much better the photograph therefore from which we can see at least what the original was actually like. But throughout the march of history these disappearances have taken place, and mankind has been fated to see vanish into the dust of the ages those material links of stone, wood and metal which bind it to its past.

It is obvious that to the European the destruction or the maiming of so many of his monuments and buildings of history or of art is tragic in a more personal way than it can ever be to an American, no matter how deeply or keenly the American, too, may react to this tragedy. The European grew up with these monuments. It was a matter for him of almost daily contact and association with them. They were woven into the very woof of his existence from the days of his earliest childhood and were the visible bridge leading from his cultural past into the present. They gave him a more immediate sensation also of being an extension of that past, a European in the finest sense of the word. Who living in places like Rouen, Coventry, Hildesheim or Pisa could escape it! They stimulated his civic pride, and won for themselves his intimate love and respect. Two recent episodes might be cited:

When, late in the spring of 1945, the famous bronze equestrian statue of Cosimo de' Medici by Gian da Bologna was returned to Florence from its temporary hiding place at Poggio a Cajano through the initiative of the Monuments and Fine Arts officer attached to Fifth Army AMG, a Florentine cabby, who happened to be crossing the Piazza della Signoria as the truck bearing the statue was entering the piazza, stood up in his cab, snapped his whip, and shouted at the top of his lungs: *Ben tornato, Cosimo!* (Welcome home, Cosimo!)

Early in 1946, the Commanding General of the American Forces in Austria made an impromptu speech at the inauguration exercises of the newly founded Austro-American Society in the Brahmssaal at Vienna. The audience sat in respectful silence as the Commanding General touched on the measures he had taken to alleviate the food and transportation problems in the American Zone in Austria. But when he mentioned the fact that he had brought back to Vienna its displaced art treasures, and particularly when he mentioned that just the day previous he had returned to Vienna the Crown Jewels and Coronation Regalia of the Holy Roman Empire, the symbols of Austrian sovereignty, the audience broke into sustained applause.

How deep the feeling of Europeans is for their art heritage was amply demonstrated in Rome, Venice, Siena, and Vienna by the native populations who—many with tears in their eyes— flocked to the exhibitions of their national and local art sponsored by the Allied Military Governments. And yet these masterpieces had been removed from public view for only the short space of six years.

The loss or destruction of these prized heritages of the past becomes in fact a personal loss comparable to that of a friend. Nor is it merely the material object that is gone, but all the values of human endeavor and beauty transmitted by them, which must henceforth be kept alive by the ghostly image in the memory or by the record of a photograph, both of which fade out with time.

The spectacle of man's destructive fury against himself and his achievements lies spread before us.

Ernest T. DeWald, Princeton University

(Lieutenant Colonel AUS, director Monuments, Fine Arts, and Archives Subcommission in Italy and Austria, Second World War.)

EDITOR'S PREFACE

WHEN I WAS first approached by the publishers and discussed with them the idea of making a book showing the main works of art and architecture that have vanished during the war, in order to preserve at least the image of many sights gone forever, little did any of us realize the extreme difficulty of the task. To begin with, as a very necessary preliminary, an authoritative and dependable list of the most important losses had to be established. For this, the Roberts Commission in Washington was an invaluable help. The Commission, however, does not cover all the countries represented in the book. In many cases, eyewitnesses who had visited destroyed regions and cities, were called upon; often their information was contradictory and confusing. Much of our information was secured through the systematic study of Signal Corps or Air Reconnaissance photographs of destroyed areas. Through careful comparison with photographs or maps of the same cities in their former state, these proved to be one of the most reliable and fruitful sources of information. Everything was done to check and recheck the information gathered, in order to reduce to a minimum the chance of error.

Having thus first established what was lost, as well as the extent of the damage, the next step was to hunt—there is no other word for it—hunt for photographs of the vanished monuments and cities. Every conceivable source was canvassed. One of the chief obstacles was the extreme difficulty of corresponding with some parts of Europe. For instance, in an attempt to get photographs of the large North German cities, we finally, in June, got in touch with the director of the Hamburg Museum. Here is a quotation from his letter, which shows the difficulties, but also proves the urgent necessity of our undertaking: "Alas, I cannot help you, much as I would wish to. Even the simplest thing is impossible: as a German I cannot send a photograph to America. But even if I could, I would not know how to get the photographs. Yes, if I still had my collection of reproductions, but they have vanished in Berlin. The good photographer in Lübeck lost all his plates in a bombing raid. Renger, who had made the best photographs of Hamburg, has been completely bombed out in Essen. I see that you have no idea of the actual state of affairs." This is only a sample of many similar letters received from Europe.

Fortunately, a number of excellent refugee photographers from Europe were found in this country. We were able for instance to draw upon a superb collection of photographs taken by a former resident of Cologne, now living in New York. Another source were the collections of museums and art historians, which have been widely used. Hundreds of photographs in scores of collections were carefully looked over to find the picture which was needed. One experience will serve to show the difficulties encountered. After looking through a number of collections, no satisfactory photograph of one of the most famous monuments on our list could be found, the Santa Trinità bridge in Florence. Pictures there were of this bridge, to be sure, but they were either old faded prints, or they gave no idea of the salient features of this wonderful monument. By the merest chance, and at the very last moment, a large collection of remarkable 'before-and-after' photographs of Florence turned up in New York, from which we were finally able to make a satisfactory choice.

The French Government sent a collection of pictures of what they considered their main losses, through the *Direction des Beaux Arts.* The same cooperation was received from the

Belgian Government. In Holland, we were able to get in touch with the *Lichtbeelden Instituut* in Amsterdam, through a friend, and by this means got practically all the documents required. With England, the problem of getting photographs was not easy. The *Historical Monuments Record,* in London, with whom we were in close touch, reported great difficulties, and that in some cases the photographs were actually non-existent, due to loss of films, along with the monuments themselves.

Photographs of even the most famous Russian monuments appeared at first to be practically non-existent, and accurate information regarding them was extremely difficult to get at. The *Sovfoto Agency* in New York seemed to be the only source of supply. Fortunately we were able to supplement these from an excellent source in Philadelphia; and the list was checked by Metropolitan Benjamin, titular Bishop of the Orthodox Church in America. But some important subjects still are lacking, such as St. Sophia of Novgorod, and the XVIIth century baroque palaces of Kiev.

With Poland, the great problem again was getting information. It was known of course that Warsaw was totally destroyed, but very meagre information could be gathered about the other cities. It is, however, comforting to know that Cracow, one of Poland's oldest and most beautiful cities, is practically intact.

Greece is not represented in the book because war damage to monuments there was comparatively negligible; none are known to have been totally destroyed.

As to Italy, the documents came from museum or private collections, and also from the Italian Government. The information on war damage in Italy is very complete, due to the excellent work of the Monuments and Fine Arts officers there, and also from such publications as the Report of the MacMillan Commission in England.

The most exciting moment, perhaps, in the preparation of the book, was the arrival at the eleventh hour of about 100 photographs from the famous Archives in Marburg, Germany, which enabled us to fill many a lacuna which might otherwise have remained unfilled.

It must be added that the scope of the book has not permitted us to be all-inclusive. Many monuments which are seriously damaged are not included simply because they are not completely destroyed, and are being or will be repaired. In this respect, certain inconsistencies may be noted, because it was felt essential to include some of these partly damaged buildings on account of the publicity which attended the damage they suffered. Such for instance is the case of San Lorenzo-fuori-le-Mura at Rome, and the Residenz at Würzburg; but in every case the exact condition has been given in the descriptive text. In a few cases, pictures of ruins have been included by way of additional information or commentary. As noted above, some things are missing simply because no photograph was available; also, a process of selection and elimination had to be adhered to, in order to keep the book within reasonable limits. But a conscientious effort has been made to represent every major destroyed monument or city, and at the same time to give each country its due, so as to present as true and reliable a picture as possible of the LOST TREASURES OF EUROPE.

Henry La Farge

ACKNOWLEDGEMENTS

THIS VOLUME is the result of the active cooperation of a great many individuals and organizations who contributed invaluable information and photographic material. In the first instance, the data on which the book is based was in large part secured from the Military Government reports of Monuments and Fine Arts officers in both the American and British armies. Their first-hand, detailed and accurate accounts of war damage constitute the most reliable available source of information for the areas under their control. To these men in particular, and to the "American Commission for the Protection and Salvage of Artistic and Historic Monuments in War Areas" (i.e., Roberts Commission) who made the reports available, the Editor is deeply indebted. In the latter connection, Mr. Charles H. Sawyer, Secretary of the Commission, and Mr. William L. M. Burke were particularly helpful and cooperative.

The greatest service was rendered by Major Bancel LaFarge, officer of Military Government, Germany, who was instrumental in securing the photographs from Germany. Signor Vittorio Ivella, Cultural Attaché of the Italian Embassy in Washington, as well as Professor Rufus Morey, U.S. Cultural Attaché in Rome, should both be mentioned in connection with the loan of photographs from the Italian Government. The editor wishes to acknowledge the receipt of continuous and valuable advice as well as material from Dr. Richard Offner, Institute of Fine Arts, N.Y.U. Grateful acknowledgements are likewise due to Professor Ernest T. DeWald, Princeton, for his extreme kindness in reviewing the section on Italy. To Horace Jayne, Vice-Director of the Metropolitan Museum of Art, and to Arthur Pope, Acting Director of the Fogg Museum of Art, special thanks are due for extending the facilities of their institutions. To Mr. Cecil Farthering, of the National Buildings Record in London, and to M. Perchet, Directeur du Service d'Architecture, in Paris, sincere acknowledgement is made for exertions in our behalf.

To all those who by constant and invaluable assistance made the publication of this book possible, the deep appreciation of the editor is expressed, and in particular to the following:

Mr. J. L. N. O'Loughlin and Mrs. Penelope Ward, British Information Services; Miss Helen Roeder, London; Mr. Jan Albert Goris, The Belgian Information Center; Mr. M. M. Lourens, The Netherlands Information Bureau; Mr. Stanislaus Centkiewicz, Editor, The Polish Review; Professor Kenneth J. Conant, Harvard University; Mr. Lamont Moore, National Gallery of Art; Miss Alice Franklin, Metropolitan Museum of Art; Mr. Girolamo Vitelli, Italian Consulate in New York; Professor Rensselaer W. Lee, Princeton University; Mrs. Corliss Lamont, National Council for American Soviet Friendship; Mr. Alexander Portnoff, American-Russian Institute in Philadelphia; Mr. Stephen Vickers, Cambridge; Miss Sylvia Széchenyi, Washington, D.C.; Sgt. Gordon Chadwick, U.S. Army.

Mr. William B. Van Nortwick, Mr. James J. Rorimer, Mr. Frederick Hartt, and Mr. Perry Cott, formerly Fine Arts officers in the American Army, were very helpful on their return with information, advice and photographic material.

Special acknowledgement should be made of the great service rendered by the continuous collaboration of Dr. Guido Schoenberger of New York University, particularly in connection with the text on the monuments in Germany, which is entirely due to him. Mlle. Hélène Barland in like manner collaborated on the text for France, as did Mrs. Irena Piotrowska for the section on Poland, and Mrs. Vera K. Ostoia for Russia.

Many other persons might be mentioned who by their help and encouragement helped to make the book possible.

Following is the list of institutions who contributed photographs: American Council of Learned Societies; American-Russian Institute, Philadelphia; Avery Library, Columbia University; Brooklyn Museum (Goodyear Collection); Fogg Museum of Art; Germanic Museum, Harvard University; Institute of Fine Arts, New York University; A. Kingsley Porter Collection; Metropolitan Museum of Art; Ministerio della Pubblica Istruzione, Rome; Yale University Gallery of Fine Arts. Following are firms and individuals who furnished photographs:

Fratelli Alinari: 113, 115, 117, 118, 119, 120, 124, 127, 128, 133, 135, 137, 140, 141, 142, 144, 145, 147, 149, 152, 155, 156, 157, 158, 159, 163, 166, 167, 169, 170, 171, 173, 174, 176, 182, 183, 186, 187, 188, 189, 190, 194, 195, 196, 198, 199, 201, 207, 209, 210

Anderson: 179, 211, 212, 213, 214, 215, 216, 217

Archives Photographiques des Monuments Historiques, Paris: 221, 222, 223, 224, 235, 236, 239, 242, 243, 245, 246, 247, 248, 249, 252, 254, 255, 258, 268, 269, 273, 274, 275, 276, 279, 280, 283, 285, 287, 288, 291

Belgian Information Center: 49, 50, 51, 56

Black Star Publishing Company: 25, 205

Tet Borsig: 148, 164

British Combine Photos, Ltd.: 93, 95, 96, 97, 416

British Information Services: 86, 88, 89, 91, 92, 94, 100, 101, 102, 103, 104

Brogi: 134, 139, 143, 146, 150, 151, 165, 168, 172, 197, 200, 202

Samuel Chamberlain: 293

Gifford Cochran: 75, 78

Compagnie Aérienne Française: 256, 270

Croci: 178

Joseph Ellner: 5, 14, 15, 19, 22

Emilia: 184, 185, 203, 208

Herbert Felton, London: 84, 87

Stadt Archiv, Freiburg (Baden): 356

French Press and Information Service: 233

Frick Art Reference Library: 160

Giraudon: 284, 289

Helen Glassner: 358

Gabriel D. Hacket: 294, 424

Lindsley F. Hall: 109, 110, 153, 282, 411, 413

Fritz Henle: 354

W. Huchthauser: 253

Hungarian Legation, Washington, D.C.: 425, 426, 427

Istituto Italiano d'Arte Grafiche: 136

Landesamt für Denkmalpflege: 345, 346, 347, 348, 349, 350, 357, 359, 360

Charles F. Leirens: 370

Fred Lewis: 90

Lichtbeelden Instituut, Holland: 32, 33, 35, 36, 38, 39

Life Magazine: 406

F. S. Lincoln: 227, 238, 240

Fred Lynn: 392, 393

Foto Marburg: 229, 230, 296, 298, 308, 309, 310, 311, 314, 320, 322, 323, 324, 327, 328, 329, 330, 336, 337, 338, 341, 342, 351, 352, 363, 364, 365, 366, 368, 384, 385, 386A, 386B, 387

Francis G. Mayer: 421

Miss Ursula Meyer: 401

Mieusement: 261, 272

Moscioni: 131, 132

Ernest Nash: 125, 129

National Buildings Record, London: 105, 106, 107, 108

National Council for American-Soviet Friendship: 83

Netherlands Information Bureau: 24, 26, 27, 28, 29, 30, 31, 34, 37, 40, 41, 42, 43, 44, 45

Neurdein: 265, 266, 267

A. Noack: 191

Vannini Parenti, Florence: 150, 151, 152

Capt. A. S. Pennoyer: 154

Mrs. Irena Piotrowska: 7, 8, 9, 12, 21

Pix Inc.: 3

Parish Church of St. Andrew, Plymouth, England: 85

Polish Review, Inc.: 6, 10, 11, 13, 16, 17, 18, 20, 23

James J. Rorimer: 228

John D. Schiff: 297, 300, 301, 302, 303, 304, 305, 307

Sommer: 123

Sovfoto Agency, New York: 60, 63, 64, 65, 66, 69, 70, 81

Three Lions: 321, 339, 340, 380, 412

U.S. Army Signal Corps: 116, 130, 271, 332, 355, 371, 373, 390, 396, 417

Clarence Ward: 225, 226, 241, 244, 257

DESCRIPTIVE LIST OF PLATES

POLAND

1. DANZIG. The *City Hall,* a brick Gothic structure begun in 1379, to which was added, in 1561, the soaring Renaissance tower. Within, a sumptuous interior called the Roter Saal dates from the same period as the tower. (Whole building destroyed.)

2. DANZIG. The *Arsenal,* one of the most remarkable and mature examples of Renaissance brick architecture in northern Europe, built in 1605 by the Flemish architect Anton van Obbergen. (Destroyed.)

3. DANZIG. Perhaps no city of Europe had preserved its mediaeval aspect to such a degree as Danzig, where picturesquely gabled houses and winding streets clustered around the massive pile of *St. Mary's Church.* A Gothic brick hall church of imposing dimensions, St. Mary's was founded in 1343, enlarged in the following century. (Almost the whole of Danzig, together with its principal monuments, was completely destroyed.)

4. DANZIG. The *Old Water Front,* showing to the left the Natural History Society Building, erected 1597–99, with the Frauentor or Gateway of Our Lady immediately adjacent. To the right, the Krahntor, with an unusually well-preserved crane dating from 1444. (Whole area ruined.)

5. DANZIG. *Warehouses* (ca. XIV century) which were the granaries used in the trade which raised Danzig to a dominant position in the Hanseatic League. (Destroyed.)

6. WARSAW. The mediaeval houses in the *Old Market Square* received during the Renaissance and baroque periods numerous superstructures and gables which imparted to them a specifically Polish character. (Completely ruined.)

7.-8. WARSAW. *St. John's Cathedral,* the most ancient church in the city, with a nave dating from the XIV century, was substantially reconstructed in 1837–41. The façade, in the English Gothic perpendicular style, was added at that time. (Completely destroyed.)

9. WARSAW. The *Old Market Square,* a survival from the original fortified city built in the XIII century, was surrounded by ancient houses. Some of these, like that of the dukes of Mazovia, dated back to the XIV century, but most of them were rebuilt after the fire of 1607, in the Renaissance and baroque style. (Completely ruined.)

10. WARSAW. The *ruins of the Old Market Square* show the general condition to which most of Warsaw has now been reduced.

11. WARSAW. The *Fukier House,* on the Old Market Square, was built in 1610 by a wealthy wine merchant. While the façade was remodelled in the XVIII century, the interior, with vaulted halls and cellars, and an arcaded court, still retained its Renaissance character. (Destroyed.)

12.-13. WARSAW. *Lazienki Palace.* King Stanislaus August Poniatowski (1764–95) was a great patron of the arts, and his reign witnessed the development of a distinct style of architecture. One of the best examples of this is the Lazienki Summer Palace, built by the architect Domenico Merlini 1784–88, where the blending of Louis XVI and Palladian elements achieved a perfect unity. (Partially destroyed; interior ruined.)

14. WARSAW. The *Krasinski Palace,* built in 1692, was a splendid example of Polish baroque palaces. (Destroyed.)

15. WARSAW. *Castle Square,* or Sigismund Square, on which was situated the former Royal Castle (right), constructed originally by the dukes of Mazovia in the XIV century. It was rebuilt early in the XVII century by King Sigismund III, who moved Poland's capital from Cracow to Warsaw. Facing the castle stands King Sigismund's column, erected by his son King Vladyslaus in 1644. (All buildings totally destroyed.)

16. WARSAW. The *Hall of Audiences* in the Royal Castle represents one of the numerous magnificent interiors added toward the end of the XVIII century. (Totally destroyed.)

17. WARSAW. The *Ball Room,* the largest and most sumptuous interior in the *Royal Castle,* was constructed in 1781 after designs by Domenico Merlini. (Destroyed.)

18. WARSAW. *Staszic Palace*, built in 1820 by Stanislaus Staszic for the Society of the Friends of Learning, after designs by Antonio Corazzi. Staszic, often called the "Patriarch of Polish Democracy," was president of the Society. (Completely destroyed.)

19. WARSAW. *St. Anne's Church*, formerly the church of the Bernardine monks, built in 1454, originally Gothic, was reconstructed in 1749 in the late baroque style. (Destroyed.)

20. WARSAW. *Church of the Holy Virgin*, said to have been built on the site where a pagan temple once stood, was founded in 1409 by Anne Januta Kiejstut, duchess of Mazovia. The massive belfry, added in 1479, is characteristic of Polish Gothic. (Destroyed.)

21. PLOCK. *The Cathedral*, built originally in the XII century, still retained its Romanesque character in spite of reconstructions in the XV and XVIII centuries. In it are tombs of Polish dukes and of Kings Ladislaus and Boleslav, of the XI and XII centuries. (Seriously damaged; in part ruined.)

22. LWOW. The *Church of the Bernardine Monks*, begun in 1600 by the most famous Lwow architect of that time, Paul of Rome, represents the flower of early baroque architecture in Poland. The church, with its cloister, was once used as a fortification. (Destroyed.)

23. POZNAN. One of the oldest cities in Poland, became, in 966, the center of Christianity in the country and for a long time was the only bishopric. The *Cathedral*, with a XIV century Gothic interior and a XVIII century exterior, was built on the spot where an earlier church had stood, dating back to the X century. To the left, St. Mary's Church (1432–44) and the Psalterium (1512). (Substantially destroyed.)

HOLLAND

24.-27. ROTTERDAM. The "Groote Kerk," or *Church of St. Lawrence* (plate 24), a vast brick Gothic edifice begun in 1412, with a choir of 1487 and an unfinished tower dated 1449–1651, was the principal landmark in the old section of Rotterdam. Although the tower still stands, the church itself has been in large part ruined; its interior, with a remarkable XVIII century choir grille (plate 26), completely destroyed by fire. All the surrounding area was completely levelled (plate 25).

The picturesque old houses along the *Steiger*, inland quay of the old port (plate 27), no longer stand.

28. HEUSDEN. This late Gothic *Town Hall* is a characteristic example of the Dutch stone and brick construction, with its traditional use of turrets and gables. (Completely destroyed.)

29. MIDDELBURG. The *Military Hospital*, fine early XVII century building, formerly the Guildhall of the Corporation of Archers. (About one half of Middelburg was destroyed, including this beautiful house.)

30. MIDDELBURG. The *Abbey of St. Nicholas*, once a rich and powerful *Praemonstratensian* house, founded in 1128 by monks from Antwerp, was secularized in 1559. Its steeple, known as the "Lange Jan," built originally in the XIII century, was rebuilt early in the XVIII century after a fire. (The tower with both churches, and houses adjacent are completely ruined.)

31. MIDDLEBURG, capital of Zeeland province, once a fortified city, was renowned in the Middle Ages for its cloth industry. Its late Gothic *Town Hall*, a symbol of the town's prosperity, was built in 1600 by Anthony Keldermans of Malines, and has an exterior decorated with colossal statues of the counts and countesses of Zeeland and Holland. (Although severely damaged, its interior completely gutted, the building will be restored.)

32. MIDDLEBURG. In a town architecturally rich in notable houses, the so-called *De Steenrots House*, built in 1590, displays the finest qualities of the Renaissance in Holland. (Completely destroyed.)

33. SLUIS, an ancient fortified city, was formerly a seaport on the Zwyn, until its harbor became filled up with sand in the XV century. In the previous century, when the harbor was still an open roadstead capable of holding large fleets, it was on June 24, 1340, the site of the great seafight between Edward III of England and the French Fleet. The magnificent *Town Hall*, shown here, with its turreted belfry, was built in 1396. (Largely ruined.)

34. ARNHEM, from 1233 to 1538 the residence of the dukes of Guelders, and one of the most attractive towns in Holland, held municipal rights as early as the XIII century, and in 1343 joined the Hanseatic League. (The whole town has been very badly damaged.)

35. ARNHEM. The "Groote Kerk," or *St. Eusebius' Church*, a late Gothic structure with a re-

markable western tower 318 ft. high, was built in 1425. (The edifice was very badly damaged, much beyond repair, and the tower in large part destroyed.)

36. VENLO. The north nave and apse of *St. Martin's,* a triple-nave Gothic hall church begun in the XIII century and completed in the XV century, is shown here. (The church was gutted and most of the apse vaulting has collapsed.)

37. RHENEN. The impressive late Gothic tower (1492–1513) of the *Church of St. Cunera* belongs to a type which is an essential feature of the Dutch landscape. (Many such towers, including the above, have been destroyed.)

38.-39. OIRSCHOT. The Collegiate *Church of St. Peter,* dating from the XV century, containing notable choir stalls of the XVI century. (Church seriously damaged by shells and gutted; tower razed; choir stalls destroyed by fire.)

40.-41. WOUWA. *St. Lambert's Church* dating from the beginning of the XV century and possessing richly carved XVII century choir stalls by A. Quellinus, said to have been brought from an abbey in Antwerp. (Burnt out, including stalls. Tower and western end destroyed.)

42. NYMEGEN. *Town Hall* (1554), an architectural masterpiece of the late Renaissance in Holland, displaying the subtle elegance characteristic of the period. The façade is adorned with statues of the emperors who were benefactors of the city. In this building was signed the Peace of Nymegen in 1679. (Destroyed.)

43. NYMEGEN. The *Weigh House,* dated 1612, situated at one end of the Market Place, appears to have been built by the same architect who built the gable of the adjacent Kerkpoort, or City Gate, shown in plate 45. (Destroyed.)

44. NYMEGEN, founded by the Romans, is the oldest and most historic town in Holland. *St. Stephen's Church,* consecrated in 1272, completed in the XV century, contains the tomb of Catherine of Bourbon, wife of Adolph of Egmont, Duke of Guelders. (The church is in large part destroyed, including the steeple.)

45. NYMEGEN. The *City Gate,* actually called the Kerkpoort, with Gothic vaulting, was built in 1545, to serve as a passage or porch giving access to St. Stephen's Church. In 1606, the remarkable gable was added, an eloquent proof of the inventiveness of Dutch Renaissance architects. This superstructure closely resembles the Danzig Armory, shown on plate 2. (Destroyed.)

46.-47. HOOGSTRATEN. In 1520 Count Lalaing-Hoogstraeten and his wife founded the flamboyant, late Gothic *Church of St. Catherine.* This impressive church contained beautiful stained glass and fine stalls. (Tower and church completely destroyed.)

48. HOOGSTRATEN. The *Town Hall,* a Gothic stone and brick structure of the late XVI century, in the characteristic style of the region. (Totally demolished.)

49. NIVELLES. The town owes its origin to a convent founded here in 645 by Ita, wife of Pepin of Landen, whose daughter, St. Gertrude, was its first abbess. The present *Church of St. Gertrude* was consecrated in 1046, in a style related to the culmination of the Cluniac Renaissance. The cloister, not quite as old as the church, represents substantially the original structure. (Cloister largely destroyed; church severely damaged.)

50. NIVELLES. The *Reliquary of St. Gertrude,* belonging to the treasure of the Collegiate Church of St. Gertrude, is the earliest and also the most remarkable example of Flemish Gothic goldsmith's work. Executed in 1272–98, it represents a Gothic church with bas-reliefs illustrating the life and miracles of the Saint. (Destroyed.)

51. BOCHOLT. The *Tree of Jesse,* detail of an early XVI century reredos of carved wood in the church at Bocholt. (Destroyed by fire.)

52. AERSCHOT. *Convent building of the Beguines,* a lay order founded by Lambert le Bègue in 1170, which still flourishes in Belgium. (Building gutted and partly destroyed.)

53. LOUVAIN. The XIV century *Church of St. Gertrude,* a Benedictine foundation, had choir stalls which were amongst the finest specimens of Gothic wood-carving in Belgium, executed by Mathias de Wayer of Brussels (ca. 1550). (Almost entirely destroyed.)

54. BASTOGNE. *St. Peter's Church* (XII-XVI century), an interesting church with Romanesque tower, contained curious XV century vaulting and ancient mural paintings. (Edifice destroyed.)

55.-56. TOURNAI. Besides various Romanesque and Gothic structures, rare survivals of the Middle Ages, the civic architecture of Tournai was remarkably rich in monuments of the succeeding centuries, due in large part to the building activity which followed the conquest of the city by Louis XIV in 1667. Under his rule, an enlightened city plan was vigorously carried out, which gave the ultimate character to the city. (Whole sections of the old town were destroyed, but the Cathedral itself was spared. Plate 56 shows destroyed area surrounding the choir of the cathedral.)

57. TOURNAI. The so-called *Maisons Romanes*, unique examples of XII century civic architecture, show a curious type of construction, reinforced with courses of stone immediately above and below each window. The windows themselves are each lightened by a graceful column. (Both houses destroyed.)

58. TOURNAI. Well-preserved and graceful XVII *century house*, the characteristic Louis XIV style of Tournai. The top story and balustrade were added in the XVIII century. (This house and many others like it were entirely destroyed.)

59. TOURNAI. The *Church of Saint-Brice*, the earliest historical mention of which is 1054, was rebuilt in the XII century and restored again subsequently. Near St. Brice was discovered, in 1653, the famous Merovingian Treasure of Childeric I (d. 481), which gives rise to the belief that St. Brice is a foundation reaching back to the V century. (Church gutted.)

RUSSIA

60. NOVGOROD. The *"Granovity" Palace*, built about 1436, forming a part of the archbishop's palace, was a hall where the archbishops received the homage of the people after their election. (Destroyed.)

61. NOVGOROD. The *Kremlin* is mentioned for the first time in 1044 as a "stone city built under Yaroslav." In the great square within these walls and towers dating from the XII-XV centuries, the popular assemblies for the election of mayors were held. (Destroyed in part.)

62. NOVGOROD. The *Spas Nereditsky Church*, or Church of the Transfiguration, built in 1198, shows the early Novgorod type of architecture which, by a simplification of the sumptuous Byzantine tradition of Kiev and Constantinople, shows an adaptation to local conditions. (Completely destroyed.)

63.-66. NOVGOROD. On the inner walls of the *Spas Nereditsky Church* a cycle of fresco paintings, done at practically the same time as the original structure (1199) and remarkably well preserved, were the most celebrated survivals of ancient Russian painting. In accordance with the Byzantine tradition of mosaic decoration, the Orante Madonna (plate 65) was situated in the apse. (Completely destroyed.)

67. PSKOV. The *Pogankiny Palaty (Mansion)* was the house of an immensely rich merchant, comprising a warehouse, a store, and the residence proper. First mentioned in 1645 (and thus a structure of the late XVI or early XVII century) it represents a type of fortified building, with very thick walls, and vaulted halls in the two lower floors. (Completely gutted.)

68.-70. ISTRA. Voskrensky Monastery, called the *New Jerusalem Monastery*, was founded by Patriarch Nicon in 1658. The Church of the Resurrection in this monastery was modelled on the Church of the Holy Sepulchre at Jerusalem, thereby constituting a departure from the traditional Russian pattern of five cupolas. The original dome having collapsed in the XVIII century, a new one (plate 68) was built, possibly after designs by B. Rastrelli. (Monastery totally destroyed.)

71. VOLOKOLAMSK. *Assumption Monastery*, founded by St. Joseph of Volotzk in 1479 in the region of Moscow. The monastery was for the most part rebuilt in the XVII century, its wealth and the sumptuousness of its architecture resulting from its location on the east-west commercial thoroughfare. Plate 71 shows the Southern Gate Church dated XVI century. (Gutted and partly destroyed.)

72.-73. PETERHOF. The *Great Palace*, begun by Peter the Great in 1715 from the plans of J.-B. Leblond, was intended as an imitation of Versailles. From the terrace, about 40 feet high, formed by the natural slope of the ground toward the Neva Bay, a huge cascade rushes down into a great pool, over steps of colored marble flanked by gilded statues and vases. Additions to the palace (plate 73) made subsequently by Empress Elizabeth show the introduction of Russian elements in the architecture. (Palace and grounds totally ruined.)

74.-76. DYETSKOYE-SELO. The *Catherine Palace*, also known as the Elizabeth Palace, was built during the latter's reign, in the years 1749-56. The principal architect was B. Rastrelli the Younger. In the fusion of the Italian, German and Russian baroque, in the excessive profusion of color and ornament, of costly materials gathered from every corner of the globe, this astonishing building sums up the magnificence and utter extravagance of the court of Elizabeth Petrovna. (Completely ruined.)

77. DYETSKOYE-SELO. *Alexander Palace*, built by Catherine the Great for her favorite grandson, later Emperor Alexander I. The building, erected between 1792-96, by Giacomo Quarenghi, is representative of the style and spirit of the reign of Catherine. The classical "Roman" revival in architecture reflects the change of mood at the court. (Ruined.)

78. LENINGRAD. General view of the *Winter Palace*, with the *Admiralty* in the distance, from a photograph taken in 1936. The Winter Palace, built by Rastrelli during the reign of Elizabeth, covers an area of approximately 23 acres. The Admiralty, with its spire, a landmark in the city, was built 1806–10, a pure example of the "Alexandrian Empire" style. (Both buildings severely damaged, but being restored.)

79. NOVGOROD. The *Yuriev Monastery* had three churches, of which the *St. George's Cathedral*, built in 1119–30, is contemporaneous with the Cathedral of St. Sophia of Novgorod. (Partly destroyed.)

80. CHERNIGOV. *Spaso-Preobrazhensk Cathedral* (i.e., Cathedral of the Transfiguration), built by Mstislav Chermny, son of St. Vladimir, around 1031. One of the very early examples in Russia of pure Byzantine architecture, of the Comnen period, it was also the best preserved. (Destroyed.)

81.-83. KIEV. The *Pechersk Lavra Monastery*, or Monastery of the Catacombs, was the great pilgrimage shrine of Russia, because the relics of the early Russian saints were preserved there, in caves overlooking the Dnieper. The principal church of the monastery, the Cathedral of the Assumption, founded by Saints Anthony and Theodosius in 1074, and built on the Byzantine plan, though considerably altered subsequently, was one of the most magnificent monuments in Russia. (Completely destroyed.)

ENGLAND

84. CANTERBURY. The *Precincts* are the extensive monastic buildings adjoining the Cathedral. The Benedictine monastery founded by St. Augustine was enlarged and converted into a priory by his successor Lanfranc, who at the same time rebuilt the Cathedral. Lanfranc was in turn succeeded by Thomas Becket, whose death was commemorated by the great pilgrimages to Canterbury, celebrated in literature by Chaucer's "Canterbury Tales." (Precincts severely damaged and in part destroyed.)

85. PLYMOUTH. *St. Andrew's Church*, built in the early xv century on a plan reminiscent of the Gothic hall church, is one of the longest parish churches in the country. Aisles running the whole

length are supplemented by short additional aisles on north and south, giving a transeptal effect in plan. The fine interior is due in large measure to the continuous barrel roof, and the Gothic arcade resting upon carved granite capitals and shafts. (Roof destroyed and whole interior ruined by fire. Masonry still standing.)

86. EXETER. *Old Houses* in High Street, finely preserved and characteristic examples of the Tudor xvi century town house, with overhanging stories, leaded casements, and interiors that mark a beginning of domestic comfort. (Houses destroyed.)

87. EXETER. On the site of the *Cathedral* stood originally a Benedictine monastery and church founded by King Athelstan, ca. 932. The Cathedral, though begun in 1112, was almost entirely rebuilt in 1280–1369 during the best years of the decorative style. This period did not produce a more noble perspective of lines than the marvelously conceived vaulting of Exeter Cathedral, with its sets of ribs spreading out as they soar upwards toward the summit of the arch. View shows choir looking east toward main altar. (Three bays of choir demolished; part of south choir aisle and St. James' Chapel at right, destroyed.)

88. LONDON. *Chelsea Old Church* with chancel and chapels at the east end dating from the xiii-xvi century, was rebuilt at the west end in 1667–70, at which time the tower also was built. No subsequent alterations had been made. The church in general had retained the monuments of its historical development, which included the chapel built by Sir Thomas More, who was a regular attendant there, having settled in Chelsea in 1524. (Completely destroyed.)

89.-90. LONDON. *All Hallows, Barking*, successor of a church founded in the vii century by Bishop Erkenwald, and committed to the care of the Abbess of Barking Abbey, in Essex. In the actual church, the pillars of the nave were Norman (ca. 1087), while the rest of the beautiful interior (plate 89) and the exterior (plate 90) was largely in the perpendicular style of the late xv century. (Ruined in large part.)

91. LONDON. *St. Brides*, Fleet Street, an old church, rebuilt by Christopher Wren in 1670–84. One of Wren's finest churches, and one of the largest, in which the classical motive has reached complete maturity in the nave arcading and fully developed clearstory. The famous spire, 226 feet high, was built in 1701. (Completely ruined, except for spire, which still stands.)

92. LONDON. *St. Lawrence Jewry*, built by

Wren in 1671–80, on the site of an earlier church destroyed by the Great Fire. Contrasting with a rather elaborate interior, the plain exterior was relieved at the east end by this arrangement in which the windows were worked into a pedimented Corinthian colonnade. (Church ruined.)

93. LONDON. The *Guild Hall,* originally built in 1411–35, but several times restored, is an outstanding survival of a great civic palace, having gate tower, court, great hall, chapel, and offices. It is actually the Hall of the Corporation of the City of London, the meeting place of the multitude of City Guilds, constituting the great mediaeval organization of city life to which the development of London is largely due. The Great Hall itself had been restored by Wren after the Great Fire of 1666. The neo-Gothic façade shown here was added in 1789; finally, a complete reconstruction of the interior was carried out in 1866–70. (Completely gutted but original masonry, which antedates the Great Fire of 1666, still stands.)

94. LONDON. The Austin Friars, known as the *Dutch Church,* originally part of an Augustinian priory (1253), was given by Edward VI in 1550 to foreign Protestant refugees, but subsequently assigned exclusively to the Dutch. The nave (built 1354) with its elegant traceried windows, had survived the Great Fire of 1666, and was a rare example of Gothic work in London. (Completely destroyed.)

95.-98. LONDON. The four great *Inns of Court,* which include Lincoln's Inn, Inner Temple, Middle Temple and Gray's Inn, are amongst the most remarkable survivals of the mediaeval organization of civic life in a great modern metropolis. They originated in the XIII century, when the clergy ceased to practice law, and are voluntary legal societies which have the exclusive right of calling persons to the English bar. The complex of buildings which were built at various periods for the use of the four Inns of Court still preserve essentially the plan of an independent self-contained community of life and action.

Middle Temple Hall (plate 95) serving as the dining hall for the benchers and students of Middle Temple, is a stately Elizabethan structure of 1562–72, of the greatest elegance. In this hall Shakespeare's "Twelfth Night" was first performed in 1601. (End wall, shown here, largely demolished.)

Gray's Inn (plate 96), which takes its name from the former owners of the site, the Lords Grey de Wilton, who relinquished their ownership to the lawyers before 1370, was built around 1560.

Its great hall was also the scene of festive life in Elizabethan times. Sir Francis Bacon, who acted as its treasurer, identified himself with all its activities, and is said to have laid out its gardens. (Interior completely ruined; walls a hollow shell.)

Pump Court (plate 97), one of the finest group of chambers within the Middle Temple, was built around 1678. Its excellent red brick construction had preserved unaltered the full character of its period. (Partly ruined.)

The round chapel of the *Temple Church* (plate 98), originally the headquarters of the Knights Templars, was consecrated in 1185. Upon the dissolution of the order in 1314, it was given to the Knights of St. John of Jerusalem, from whom it ultimately came into the possession of the Inns of Court. An enlarged choir was added in 1240, but the church was poorly restored in the XIX century. (Largely ruined.)

99. LONDON. *Merchant Taylors' Hall,* the largest and one of the most splendid of the City Companies' Halls. This company was founded in 1327, and the original hall was erected in the latter part of the XIV century. Although the general structure of the Hall dates from that time, this sumptuous interior is largely a XIX century reconstruction. (Completely gutted.)

100. LONDON. *Portman House* (XVIII century). This interior is one of the masterpieces of Robert Adam, the originator of a style which in England is the counterpart of the Louis XVI style in France. The ultimate derivation of the style resides in an attempted reconstruction of classical private dwellings, of which Robert Adam made an extensive study, especially of Diocletian's Palace at Spalato. Its special characteristics are the creation of subtle oval forms, great concern for interior decoration, and the highly developed use of low-relief stucco. (House completely destroyed.)

101. LONDON. The *Charterhouse,* founded in 1371 as a priory of the Carthusians, the order founded by St. Bruno at the Grande Chartreuse, near Grenoble. Subsequent to the dissolution (1537), it became in 1611 a privately endowed hospital and retreat for the aged. Most of the buildings date from the XVI century, including its Great Hall, a masterpiece of Elizabethan woodwork. (Whole complex largely ruined, including the Great Hall.)

102. BATH. The associations of Bath with ancient Rome, and certain fragments of classical architecture found there may well have served to inspire the XVIII century builders of the resort town at an age when the classic revival was in full swing. Among these XVIII buildings is the famous *Royal Crescent* whose exceptional scale and complete unity of style were made possible by the English system of land tenure and because of the vision of its owners. (Sections of Royal Crescent ruined, but damage repairable.)

103. BRISTOL. *Berkeley Square* is another example of the late XVIII century tendency toward a harmonious development of city building, an ideal which for the most part was lost sight of during the XIX century. Berkeley Square was laid out on the outskirts of the city in 1786, and was slowly built up through the next two decades. But this row of houses nevertheless shows a complete and charming unity of style, due to carefully studied architectural relations at each successive stage. (Partly destroyed.)

104. BRISTOL. *St. Peter's Hospital,* originally a mediaeval mansion, was largely rebuilt in 1610. As such it constitutes a splendid example of the Tudor town house. Here are found all the traditional characteristics of the period in which rich decorative elements are combined with corbelled and overhanging stories and roofs, and where reigns a general atmosphere of sophisticated comfort. (Totally destroyed.)

105. BRISTOL. The *Church of St. Mary-le-Port,* a small XV century Gothic church, with fine large windows in the perpendicular style. It was noted for a fine XVIII century wooden reredos. (Church largely ruined.)

106. ETON. The *Upper School* at Eton College was erected in 1689–94 by Christopher Wren, and as such constitutes Eton's principal building of that period. The interior had retained its original panelling. (Serious damage suffered by this building as well as by Saville House, built 1603–04.)

107. NORWICH. The name of Norwich first appears in the Saxon Chronicle in 1004, and in 1094 the town became a bishopric. During the reign of Elizabeth, a large number of Dutch and Walloons settled in Norwich. They were Protestant refugees from the Spanish domination and their number increased substantially during the course of the century. This may serve to explain the definite Jacobean form of these gabled structures in the *Cathedral Close.* (Houses ruined.)

108. GREAT YARMOUTH. Detail of bas-reliefs on the vaulted ceiling of the *Grey Friars' Cloister,* the remains of a Franciscan monastery of the XIII century. (Destroyed.)

109. COVENTRY. *Ford's Hospital,* a remarkable half-timbered structure, erected in 1509–29 under the will of one William Ford. Founded as a hospital, a rather elaborate building built around an inner court, it still served its original purpose. (Largely ruined.)

110. COVENTRY. *St. Michael's Cathedral,* an impressive and splendid perpendicular Gothic edifice built 1373–94. The generous scale of the interior, with broad nave and aisles, a clearstory, and huge traceried windows was a reflection of the communal enterprise and the prosperity of the local guilds of merchants. (Completely destroyed, except for the spire which still stands.)

111. COVENTRY. In the quarter adjoining the Cathedral on the south side, was *St. Mary's Hall.* Built for the Trinity Guild between 1394–1414, it contained a large hall characteristic of the period. (St. Mary's Hall, in center, completely ruined.)

112. MANCHESTER. The *Cathedral,* dating from the XV century, a fine example of the perpendicular style. The great width of the structure is unusual and is due to double aisles, the outer ones having originally been chapels. On the north side of the choir (center in plate 112) is the Derby Chapel with remarkable carved screens and a fine XVII century Flemish altar (Derby Chapel destroyed, rest of building intact.)

ITALY

113.-114. PALERMO. *San Francesco d'Assisi,* begun in 1255, one of the many churches throughout Italy dedicated to St. Francis within the century of his death (1226) and canonization (1228). Although the general disposition of the façade (1302) is derived from the church of St. Francis at Assisi, the pointed arch and sculptural details indicate the persistence of the Norman style in Palermo. The interior, on the basilica plan, was completely remodelled in the XVII century. (Partly ruined.)

115.-120. BENEVENTO. A pre-Roman town of great antiquity, Benevento began to gain importance in 486 by its situation on the trade route to the Near East. In 571 it was a Lombard dukedom, and in the XI century it passed to the domain of the Popes. The *Cathedral,* originally of the XI century, was largely rebuilt by Cardinal Ruggiero, a monk from Monte Cassino, who had the jurisdiction of this archbishopric from 1179–1221. With the exception of the bronze doors, the façade was formed in large part from fragments of local Roman and Lombard monuments. The campanile was built in 1279 entirely of elements from Roman monuments. Although the authorship of the *Portal* (plates 117-118) is in question, the bronze work is generally attributed to Greek artists of the XI-XII century. Of the 77 panels, 44 represent scenes in the life of Christ, 24 are portraits of contemporaneous bishops. The *interior* (plate 119), originally of three naves, was enlarged by Ruggiero to five. All the columns of the central nave, together with their Doric capitals and bases, were from an unidentified Roman temple. The authorship of the *pulpit* (plate 12) is not known. (Whole edifice completely ruined, with exception of campanile.)

121. NAPLES. At *Monte Oliveto,* also called the church of Santa Anna dei Lombardi, begun in 1411, a chapel was built for the Liguoro family. Its altar, shown here, was the work of Marigliano, called Giovanni da Nola, done in 1532. (Completely destroyed except for figure of the Virgin. The Mastrogiudici and Piccolomini chapels, with famous altars by Benedetto da Maiano and by A. Rossellino, were largely destroyed, but the individual sculptures were saved.)

122. NAPLES. *Santa Maria del Carmine,* an ancient conventual church, entirely remodelled in 1769, at which time the rich coffered ceiling was installed. (Edifice gravely damaged; roof and ceiling destroyed.)

123.-124. NAPLES. *Santa Chiara.* With the conquest of Naples by Charles I of Anjou in 1266 a great revival of art and literature occurred. Norman influences soon dominated in the great building activity which followed. To this time belongs the historic church of Santa Chiara, built in 1310–24, originally a local interpretation of Norman architecture, though entirely remodelled in the baroque style in 1742–57. This church was filled with sculptured tombs of various members of the Angevine dynasty including in particular the great *Tomb of Robert the Wise,* behind the main altar. This great monument (plate 124, detail) was made by Giovanni and Pacio da Firenze around 1345. (Largely destroyed.)

125.-128. MONTE CASSINO. In 529, St. Benedict founded the *Abbey* on the site of a pagan temple, dedicating it to St. John the Baptist and St. Martin of Tours. After having been several times sacked, it enjoyed a period of comparative peace under Desiderio (1058). During this time, a new basilica, with three naves, was built. This was destroyed by an earthquake in 1349, and a reconstruction was carried out under Urban V. Except for the foundations and certain lower crypts, the extensive organism which had come down to modern times (plate 125) was largely built during the XVI and

XVII centuries. The *Central Court* (plate 127) was built in 1515 by Abbot Squarcialupi, a Florentine. In 1627 was consecrated the new church, a sumptuous edifice richly adorned in the baroque manner. Its *Sacristy* (plate 128) with wardrobes of remarkable carved woodwork, had preserved a part of the XVI century mosaic floor of Desiderio's original basilica. (Totally destroyed.)

129.-130. ROME. *San Lorenzo-fuori-le-Mura,* founded by Constantine, was in the III century one of the five patriarchal churches of Rome, all under the jurisdiction of the bishop of Rome. It was thus from the earliest time a pilgrimage church, which it has remained to this day. In 578, Pelagius III replaced the original structure with a basilica having an entrance at the east end. To this, Honorius III in 1216–27 added the present nave with a portico at the west (plate 129). The 6 columns of this portico are elements from ancient Roman buildings, as are the 22 columns within, in the nave built by Honorius. (Western façade demolished, but repairable.)

131. FRASCATI. *Villa Falconieri,* built in 1545–48. Enlarged in 1648 by the architect Francesco Borromini for Orazio Falconieri. (In part ruined; right wing destroyed.)

132. FRASCATI. *Villa Lancellotti,* originally Villa Tusculana, built in the XVI century. (Upper part of façade ruined.)

133. PALESTRINA, ancient pre-Roman city with archaeological remains dating from the VIII century B.C., is said to owe its foundation to colonists under the tutelage of Telemachus. The *Barberini Palace,* begun in 1493, was remodelled in the XVII century by the Barberini family, who acquired the tenure of Palestrina by purchase from the papacy in 1630. The palace is built on the remains of the ancient Temple of Fortuna. (Partly destroyed.)

134. VALMONTONE. The *Doria-Pamphili Palace,* built in the XVII century, country seat of a noble Roman family. Beyond the palace can be seen the dome of the Collegiate Church of Valmontone. (Both buildings largely ruined.)

135. TARQUINIA. *Vitelleschi Palace,* built in 1439 by Giovanni Vitelleschi, papal condottiere who was made cardinal in reward for his services, but who subsequently died in disgrace for abuse of power. Two distinct building periods are evident in the edifice, the earlier with Gothic windows and crenelated cornice, the later in the style of a Renaissance palace. Within is a high vaulted court leading to an open loggia overlooking the Tyrrhenian Sea. (Largely destroyed.)

136.-137. TERNI. Upon the death of St. Francis of Assisi, who had visited and preached at Terni, the *Church of San Francesco* (plate 137) was built liturgically in conformance with the original Franciscan church at Assisi, its façade having the identical disposition of rose window over the central portal, in a simple and severe style. The interior (ceiling, plate 136) was embellished in the XVII century in a manner which, although entirely out of keeping with the original spirit of the church, constitutes a remarkable example of the stucco decoration of the period, attributed to Cristoforo da Stroncone. (Whole building completely destroyed.)

138. VITERBO. *San Sisto,* the oldest church in Viterbo, originally built in the VIII century, was considerably altered in the XII century by the unusual raising of the apse. (Largely ruined.)

139.-141. VITERBO. The fact that Viterbo was the residence of the popes in the Middle Ages, and the theatre of strife between the papacy and the emperor, also between Guelf and Ghibelline, had a lasting effect on the town. During the period of peace following the death of Innocent IV in the XIII century, there was a great building activity, at which time the *Church of Santa Maria della Verità,* begun about 1240, was built. In general form, it was directly related to the rich Benedictine architecture which came to Italy from France, and it had a remarkable Gothic cloister. Within, a chapel given by Nardo Mazzatosta was in 1453 completely decorated with frescoes by *Lorenzo da Viterbo.* The vaulting of the chapel (plate 139) had representations of the Evangelists and various saints; on the walls were depicted scenes from the life of the Virgin. According to Berenson, the scene of the *Marriage of the Virgin* (plate 141) is "one of the most famous representations of the subject . . . Seldom shall you witness a more spacious ceremony than this Marriage of the Virgin, festive yet stately, filled with the majestic men, staid matrons and proud life-enjoying youth." These frescoes were the only extant paintings by Lorenzo. (Church and frescoes largely destroyed.)

142. VITERBO. The *Fountain on the Piazza della Rocca* was built in 1575 from designs by the architect Giacomo Baroccio, called da Vignola. (Destroyed.)

143. VITERBO. *San Giovanni in Zoccoli,* built around 1037, was the least altered of the old churches in Viterbo. The simple interior with its three naves retained the very essence of Tuscan Romanesque. The façade was rebuilt in the XII century. (Completely destroyed.)

144.-145. SIENA. The *Osservanza,* founded in 1423 by St. Bernardin of Siena, was enlarged in 1485 by the architect Giacomo Cozzarelli. It was noted for the purity of its early Renaissance style, with arches and vaulting decorated with terra cottas by Cozzarelli. In one of its altars was a terra cotta bas-relief by Andrea della Robbia, representing the *Coronation of the Virgin* (plate 145). (Vaulting largely destroyed; interior largely ruined, including altarpiece.)

146.-147. SAN GIMIGNANO. *Barna da Siena* is best known for his series of frescoes in the *Cathedral,* i.e., *Collegiata,* representing thirty scenes from the life of Christ. All the great qualities of the Trecento Siennese school are clearly present in these paintings, in which both the dramatic narrative form of the composition, and the rich color are reminiscent of Duccio, and of the Lorenzetti. Barna never completed the series, because of his untimely death in 1380, as described by Vasari. (Plate 146 shows the *Crucifixion,* which was ruined in the lower part, especially the central group below the Cross. The *Marriage at Cana,* plate 147, was almost totally destroyed; various others of the series were seriously damaged.)

148. BADIA A SETTIMO, founded in 908 as a Benedictine monastery, became Cistercian in 1236, at which time it assumed great importance by its cultural activities. One of its portals, the so-called *Columbaione Tower* (plate 148), was decorated with a gigantic relief of the Saviour, dating from the XIV century. (Tower completely destroyed.)

149. FLORENCE. The reestablishment of the Medici dynasty by the accession of Cosimo I brought about a new blossoming of artistic endeavor in Florence, and for a few years again the city experienced some of its former glory. During this period Cosimo undertook a series of public works, the most important of which were the Ponte Santa Trinità and the Mercato Nuovo. From the same period also dates the Lungarno Acciaioli, the spacious quay which theretofore did not exist. Along this quay is the *Palazzo Acciaioli* which had been since the XVI century the residence of the Acciaioli, a powerful mercantile and banking firm. Its fine Lungarno front, with the characteristic balcony, was added at this time. (One half of the Lungarno Acciaioli, including the palace, was completely demolished at the time of the destruction of the bridges.)

150.-152. FLORENCE. The *Santa Trinità Bridge,* the most remarkable of the Renaissance bridges in its grace and originality, was one of the outstandng public works in Florence carried out under Cosimo I. It was built in 1567–70 from designs by Bartolomeo Ammannati who invented a new form for the arches wherein the radius of the curvature decreases toward the piers until the intrados becomes vertical as it touches the side of the piers. Four statues, two at each end of the bridge, represent the four seasons. Beyond the *statue of Autumn* (plate 150) appears the Ponte alla Carraia, built 1218, restored and partly rebuilt by Ammannati in 1337. Behind the *statue of Summer* (plate 151) appears the Borgo San Jacopo, and the Ponte Vecchio. (Ponte Santa Trinità completely destroyed, as also the Ponte alla Carraia and Borgo San Jacopo.)

153. FLORENCE. *Borgo San Jacopo,* the characteristic mediaeval Arno front of Florence, including houses dating from the XIII century. (Completely destroyed.)

154. FLORENCE. View taken from the Borgo San Jacopo, looking across the Arno toward the Lungarno Acciaioli, showing ruined areas on both sides.

155.-158. IMPRUNETA. The *Collegiate Church of Santa Maria,* consecrated in 1054, rebuilt in 1593, possessed a miraculous image of the Virgin and a piece of the True Cross. In order to keep these relics fittingly, special chapels were built for them, from designs by Michelozzo. The *Chapel of the Madonna* (plate 155) was executed 1452–56, with a terra cotta frieze above, in which were inserted bas-relief plaques of the Madonna and Child (plate 156) by Luca della Robbia. In the *Chapel of the True Cross,* the figures of St. John the Baptist and St. Augustine (plate 157), together with the *Crucifixion* (plate 158), are all the work of Luca della Robbia. The latter, which includes the figures of St. John and the Virgin, is considered the most inspired work of the master. (Both chapels ruined; the sculptures severely damaged.)

159.-162. IMPRUNETA. *Collegiata.* Tommaso del Mazza and Pietro Nelli, Florentine painters, collaborated on the *polyptych* for the high altar of Santa Maria di Impruneta. The work was executed in 1375. Plate 159 shows the whole altarpiece, Plate 160 the central panel, representing the Madonna and Child surrounded by Saints. Plate 161, the Annunciation, one of the small panels at top; plate 162 one of the lower panels, representing the Ark of the Covenant. (Altarpiece destroyed by fire.)

163. EMPOLI. *Collegiata di Sant'Andrea,*

founded in the V century, rebuilt subsequently, contained many notable Tuscan paintings. Among them was the *Annunciation* attributed to *Francesco Botticini,* showing the influence of Filippino Lippi and Botticelli. (Body of church ruined, together with some of its contents, although most of the paintings had been previously removed. The Annunciation by Botticini was amongst those lost.)

164. PRATO. The *Tabernacle by Filippino Lippi* is described by Vasari as follows: "This master likewise painted a Tabernacle in fresco at the corner of the Mercatale . . . in Prato, opposite to the convent of Santa Margherita and near some houses belonging to the nuns. In this work there is an exceedingly beautiful figure of the Virgin, in the midst of a choir of seraphim; the whole group is surrounded by a brilliant light." Painted in 1498. (Destroyed.)

165. PISA. The *Ponte del Mezzo,* built in 1660, is probably derived from the Ponte Santa Trinità at Florence, but lacks the spirit of the latter. The use of white marble for the archivolts and moulded courses, however, gave it a certain elegance, and it was well designed for its setting. The large building and tower across the bridge is the *Palazzo Pretorio.* (Bridge and Palazzo Pretorio, together with the succession of palaces and houses on both sides of the Arno, largely ruined, presenting a scene of universal destruction.)

166. PISA. *Medici Palace,* situated in the Piazza Mazzini, a Gothic mansion dating from the XIII century, enlarged in the XIV. (Largely ruined.)

167. PISA. The ancient prosperity which Pisa had enjoyed as a Roman city, and had subsequently lost, was revived under Charlemagne, through whose benevolence also the *Church of San Paolo a Ripa d'Arno* was founded in 805. The present church, however, is the result of radical reconstruction in the XI-XII century. In 1148, when Pope Eugene III consecrated the main altar, the church must have attained its final form. (Body of church largely ruined.)

168.-171. PISA. *Camposanto.* The principal artist of the several who decorated the walls of the Camposanto was *Benozzo Gozzoli,* who at one time worked in the studio of Fra Angelico. Gozzoli came to Pisa in 1469, at which time he began his vast cycle of paintings representing episodes in the history of the world, mostly as related in the Old Testament. The *Tower of Babel* (plate 170), one of the best preserved of the series, is filled with people who are the spectators of that Biblical event, but who represent contemporary personages, including Cosimo de Medici and his sons. In the imaginary city depicted can be recognized famous buildings of Florence and of ancient Rome. A beautiful landscape (plate 169) fills the left side of the composition. *Noah's Vintage and Drunkenness* (plate 171) is a continuous narrative depicted within a single composition. Over the door of the Ammannati Chapel, Gozzoli painted *The Epiphany* (plate 168) and immediately below it a charming Annunciation. (All these are amongst the most seriously damaged of the series, discolored and wrecked by flame and exposure.)

172. PISA. *Camposanto*. It is generally agreed that the unknown painter of the *Triumph of Death* was probably *Francesco Traini*, a pupil of Orcagna and a native of Pisa. According to Berenson, this painting is "as mere illustration, by far the greatest Italian achievement of the Middle Ages. . . . His devils and goblins are alive and endowed with all the hard-won beauty of the true grotesque. His Death would be terrifyingly recognizable even without the bat wings and the scythe . . ." (The central part of the composition, shown here, ruined in large part.)

173. ANCONA. *Santa Maria della Verità* (1399), a Gothic church, but Romanesque in plan. The remarkable early Renaissance portal was added in the XVI century, during a period of great building activity. (Completely destroyed.)

174. FANO. The Gothic *Palazzo della Ragione*, built in 1299, was an expression of the civic pride and independence of the commune vis-à-vis the ambitions of the Malatesta. The tower was added in 1739 from designs by L. Vanvitelli. (Tower and part of building destroyed.)

175. FANO. *San Paterniano*, with the adjoining convent, was built toward the middle of the XVI century, and is generally attributed to the Venetian architect Sansovino. (Tower destroyed.)

176.-177. RIMINI. *Temple of the Malatesta*. In 1447, Sigismondo Malatesta assigned to Leon Battista Alberti the task of transforming the XIII century Gothic church of San Francesco into a monument as a thank offering for his safety during a dangerous campaign undertaken for Pope Eugenius IV around 1445. Actually it is rather a monument that perpetuates the glory of his name and of his attachment for Isotta degli Atti. Alberti conceived the splendid façade in the shape of a triumphal arch, inspired from the Arch of August at Rimini, and enveloped the whole building, inside and out, in a structure which is one of the marvels of the Italian Renaissance. The interior is

enriched with a famous fresco by Piero della Francesca, and by the inimitable bas-reliefs of Agostino di Duccio and Matteo di Pasti. The apse alone had remained in its original Gothic form. (Apse and beamed ceiling completely destroyed, but rest of structure and works of art substantially intact.)

178. FORLI. *San Biagio*. The tomb of Barbara Manfredi, wife of Pino III Ordelaffi, whose family dominated Forli from 1315 to 1480. The work was executed in 1467–80 by Francesco di Simone Ferrucci, Florentine sculptor and architect. Ferrucci ranks high amongst the Florentine artists of that period, in style being closely related to Desiderio da Settignano, whose pupil he was, and to Verrocchio. (Monument destroyed.)

179.-181. FORLI. The ceiling in the Sforza Chapel of *San Biagio* is generally jointly attributed to *Melozzo da Forli* and *Palmezzano,* due to the fact that Melozzo died in 1494, a year before the completion of the work. It is generally believed that the design and the major part of the ceiling was executed by Melozzo himself; and that his pupil Marco Palmezzano completed the work after the latter's death. Melozzo, a pupil of Piero della Francesca, abandoned the severe impersonal types of his master, changing the latter's abstract figures into terms of human grandeur, "using them always as a means for embodying emotions, so that they become pure incarnations of the one grand feeling by which they are animated." (Ceiling completely destroyed.)

182. BOLOGNA. The portal of the *Corpus Domini,* (built 1481–97), a magnificent and characteristic example of Bolognese terra cotta. It is generally attributed to Niccolo Sperandio, a famous medallist and craftsman who came to Bologna in 1478, under the patronage of Francesco Gonzaga. (Whole church ruined; façade and portal destroyed.)

183. BOLOGNA. *San Francesco* was the first church in Italy built in the pure Gothic style. Built in 1236–63 by Marco da Brescia, it is throughout a perfect imitation of the French Gothic churches, both in plan and in execution, showing a complete understanding of the northern ogival construction. (West part of church ruined, including a section of the nave; choir and apse intact.)

184.-185. BOLOGNA. The *Palazzo dell' Archiginnasio,* a splendid edifice built in 1562–63 to house the University of Bologna. The architect was Antonio Morandi, a follower of Peruzzi, Alessi and Vignola. One of the halls within, the *Anatomical Theatre,* built by Antonio Levanti in 1756, was made entirely of spruce woodwork with carved figures in niches in the walls and coffered ceiling. (Whole building severely damaged; Anatomical Theatre destroyed.)

186.-187. PARMA. The *Farnese Theatre* was built in 1618–19 from designs by Giovanni Battista Aleotti. This sumptuous theatre is reminiscent of Venetian XVI century architecture. In the use of the classical elements, the only other theatre of that period remotely comparable to it is the Teatro Olimpico at Vicenza, but the semicircular amphitheatre is unique. (Largely destroyed.)

188. GENOA. *Palazzo Negrone,* XVI century palace in the Via Garibaldi, characteristic example of Genoese baroque stucco and fresco ornament. (Façade almost completely destroyed.)

189. GENOA. *San Stefano,* one of the two oldest churches in Genoa, founded in the X century. The façade, with its alternating bands of black and white marble, dates from the XIII century. (Façade ruined, apse and campanile intact.)

190. GENOA. Among the later palaces of Genoa, the *Royal Palace* by size and beauty ranks first. Formerly named the Durazzo Palace, it was built by the architects Giovanni Antonio Falcone and Francesco Cantone, in 1650. The classical majesty of Genoese palace architecture is reflected in this magnificent interior, where the influence of Bernini is quite evident. (Interior ruined.)

191. GENOA. *Palazzo Pallavicini* belongs to a numerous group of late XVI and XVII century palaces built by followers of the tradition of Galeazzo Alessi. The structural functions of the architecture was realized either by marble pilasters and other elements, or by resorting (as here) to frescoed surfaces of simulated architecture. Palazzo Pallavicini is one of the most beautiful of this kind, with frescoes executed in 1585 by Lazzaro Calvi. (Façade severely damaged.)

192. GENOA. The basilica of *Santissima Annunziata del Vastato* (XVII century) was probably built by Giacomo della Porta, the most talented pupil of Vignola. The scheme of the columnar basilica, which was revived at this epoch, was here magnificently realized. It is one of the most splendid baroque churches in existence. (Largely ruined; right aisle completely destroyed.)

193. In Genoa, the luxuriousness and majesty of the *Via Balbi,* described by Vasari as the most resplendent street in all of Italy, in truth reflected the taste of its rich and powerful citizens. The astounding transformation of the city in the XVI and XVII centuries, with the wealth and exuberance of its palaces, was largely due to the genius of Alessandro Alessi (1512–72) and his followers. (Via Balbi largely ruined, with many of its palaces gutted and partly destroyed.)

194. TURIN. The *Palazzo dell' Università,* begun in 1713 from designs by the Genoese architect Antonio Ricca. The spacious disposition of the great court bestows on this structure the haughty proportions associated with Genoese palaces. (Half destroyed, including both monumental staircases.)

195. TURIN. The eighteenth century façade of the *Palazzo Madama,* together with its monumental stairs, was added by Filippo Juvara around 1718. By its space composition and splendid decorative effects, it stands as one of the most impressive architectural masterpieces of the XVIII century in Italy. (Interior partly ruined.)

196. MILAN. The *Ospedale Maggiore* was the first lay hospital, having been built entirely by contributions from the public. (Hospitals theretofore were founded entirely by monasteries.) A huge structure built around an inner court, it was begun in 1457 by the architect Filarete, continued by G. Solari after 1465. With the Castello Visconteo, the Ospedale Maggiore initiates the Renaissance in Milan. (Court presents vast scene of interior destruction. Exterior façade mostly standing.)

197. MILAN. The *Marino Palace,* one of the most splendid in Milan, was erected in 1558–60 by Galeazzo Alessi. Its court in particular abounds with the brilliance of Alessi's genius. (Entirely gutted; court seriously damaged.)

198. MILAN. *Santa Maria delle Grazie,* begun in 1460 by the Dominicans, was completed by Bramante around 1492. To him are due the choir, crossing, and beautiful six-sided dome, with its elegant exterior ornament in marble and terra cotta, as well as both cloisters. The large cloister, shown here, leads to the former refectory on the walls of which are Leonardo's "Last Supper" and Donato da Montorfano's "Crucifixion." (Both cloisters almost entirely destroyed; church damaged, with walls of side chapels and adjoining vaults partly demolished. Refectory completely destroyed, but both frescoes saved by protective masonry.)

199. MILAN. *Royal Palace,* occupying the site of the earlier mansions of the Visconti and Sforza, was completely rebuilt in 1771–78 by Giuseppe Piermarini. Its great hall was featured by a gallery supported by caryatids, and the ceiling had frescoes by Appiani. (Completely ruined by fire.)

200.-201. MILAN. *San Ambrogio,* founded by

St. Ambrose in the IV century, but chiefly a structure of the XII century in the form of a Romanesque basilica, is one of the most important monuments in Italy, containing structural elements from almost every period. Among these was the *Canonica* (plate 201), with its noble portico by Bramante (1492). The sacristy of the church was embellished with a ceiling fresco by *G. B. Tiepolo* (plate 200) representing the *Apotheosis of St. Bernard*. (Church intact; Bramante portico and Tiepolo ceiling destroyed. Note: Other ceilings by Tiepolo destroyed are those of Palazzo Clerici and Palazzo Archinti both in Milan, and in the Palazzo Canossa at Verona.)

202. PAVIA. The *covered bridge over the Ticino,* built 1351–56 by Jacopo Gozzo and Giovanni Ferrara, has arches in the form of flat segmented arcs similar to those of the Ponte Vecchio, in Florence, where this type was first used in the proportions of modern stone arcs. The chapel, dedicated to St. John Nepomuk, was built in the XVII century. (Almost entirely destroyed, including chapel.)

203. BRESCIA. *Salvadego Palace,* built in the XVII century, was typical of the provincial refinement and cultivation of Brescia. The palace was celebrated chiefly for the series of frescoes by Moretto da Brescia in the halls of the ground floor. (Whole building ruined, but frescoes miraculously saved.)

204. BRESCIA. *Santa Maria dei Miracoli.* The origin of the church was due to a miraculous image of the Virgin on the wall of a private house. In order to protect the image, a chapel was built, which was later transformed into this precious jewel of the Venetian-Lombard Renaissance. Begun in 1487, the existing portico was the original structure, to which in the XVI century were added the remaining parts of the façade, the lateral naves and the circular dome by Stefano Lamberti and Girolamo Pellegrino. (Church completely ruined, except for original portico which was saved by protective masonry.)

205. VERONA. The *Scaligero Bridge* over the Adige was built about 1354 to serve as a fortified entrance to the city by way of the Castel Vecchio. The span of the large arch (adjacent to the Castel Vecchio) was 160 feet, for many years the longest span in the world. (Bridge completely destroyed.)

206. VERONA. Vestiges of classical antiquity still visible in Verona in various forms are more abundant there than in almost any other city in northern Italy. Among these was the *Ponte della Pietra,* a Roman bridge, restored and strengthened

in the XV century. The mediaeval restorations are visible in the alternating bands of stone and brick. (Completely destroyed.)

207.-208. VICENZA. Few public squares of Italy are surrounded by such a remarkable aggregate of buildings as the *Piazza dei Signori,* dominated by the Basilica, Palladio's first great masterpiece (plate 207, right side). Facing the Basilica is the graceful Monte di Pietà (plate 207, left side) built in 1499–1553 and consequently one of the earliest of those "lending house" establishments, instituted and developed in Italy by the Franciscans and Dominicans for the relief of the poor. The façade of the church of San Vincenzo (plate 208), dated 1614–17, divides the façade of Monte di Pietà into two equal parts. The tall Torre dell'Orologio, and the two free-standing columns surmounted one by the Lion of St. Mark, the other by St. Theodore, dated respectively 1464 and 1640, at the extremity of the square (plate 207), add to its unusual character. (General damage throughout. Façade and arcades of Basilica partly ruined, but restorable. Monte di Pietà, roofless and suffered much interior damage, façade shell-scarred; San Vincenzo gutted; upper part of tower destroyed, etc.)

209. VICENZA. The *Palazzo da Schio,* one of the finest of the XV century Venetian Gothic palaces in Vicenza. (Half ruined: loggia on left side destroyed; portal intact.)

210. VICENZA. The *Palazzo Valmarana,* built 1566, a documented work by Palladio on the basis of his own description of it. Characteristic of his later development when, under the influence of Venice and particularly of Sansovino, he freed himself from pure classicism and showed great originality in the free use of pilasters, free-standing or engaged columns, orders running through two stories, or superimposed, sculptured ornament and so forth. (Partially destroyed, including upper part of façade and the interior.)

211.-212. RAVENNA. *Santa Maria in Porto fuori,* a basilica, founded around 1096 by Piero degli Onesti, called "Il Peccatore," a native of Ravenna who renounced his inheritance to found this church, celebrated by Dante's verses concerning it. (Almost totally destroyed.)

213.-216. PADUA. The series of frescoes in the *Ovetari Chapel of the Eremitani* were executed between 1448 and 1455. They represent chiefly scenes from the life of St. James and St. Christopher. While it is known that others collaborated with Andrea Mantegna in their execution, the general motive and unity makes it certain that

26

Mantegna was the artist who planned the whole. The particular frescoes definitely attributed to him are the *Baptism of Hermogenes* (plate 216), St. James before Herod Agrippa, *St. James being led to his Martyrdom* (plates 213 and 214) and *Death of St. James* (plate 215). Although these represent the earliest work on a large scale undertaken by Mantegna, they are manifestly the product of an independent and creative mind. It would be difficult to find another work so dramatically alive and so concentrated as these scenes from the life of St. James, so monumental and yet so human as the Baptism of Hermogenes. Andrea Mantegna, coming fifty-seven years after the death of Petrarch, was another great humanist in the great intellectual center of Padua, and one of the most gifted figures of the Renaissance. Making it breathe a new life, Mantegna freed Italian art from the limited idiom of the Middle Ages, endowing the images of the Christian world with the splendor and power of Rome. By the nobility and originality of his style, he stands at the fountainhead of all the artistic tendencies of northern Italy. (Ovetari Chapel and the whole apse of the Eremitani entirely destroyed.)

217. PADUA. *Eremitani.* The attribution of the *vaulting of the Ovetari Chapel,* with its representation of the four Evangelists, to any one artist is not possible. While the designs are believed to have been made by Mantegna, the actual execution was probably carried out by one of his collaborators, all of whom, including Mantegna himself, were pupils of Squarcione. (Destroyed.)

218. POLA. *Temple of Rome and Augustus,* an elegant and well-preserved monument, erected 2–14 B.C. It consists of a cella, and a Corinthian tetrastyle pronaos, with two columns at the sides and a magnificent frieze. (Pronaos destroyed; rest of structure still standing.)

219. POLA. The *Duomo,* originally a VI century basilica, remodelled in the XVII century, and more recently restored. View shows the old part of the nave, with early Christian elements. (Interior partly ruined.)

FRANCE

220.-222. ST. MALO became a bishopric in the XII century with the *Church of St. Vincent* as Cathedral until the see was suppressed in 1790. The picturesque Channel port and fortress was largely composed of XVII-XVIII century houses, all built of the local granite. The names of famous explorers and sailors such as Jacques Cartier, Robert Surcouf and Moreau de Maupertuis are associated with St. Malo. (The whole town is in ruins.)

223.-224. VALOGNES. Fifteenth century church with hexagonal tower and dome dated 1612, unique example of a Gothic dome in France. (Destroyed.)

225.-226. LESSAY. The *Abbey Church,* begun in the end of the XI century, completed before 1250, constitutes one of the earliest known examples of ogival ribbed vaulting. The simplicity of its plan, the great width of the nave, and the solid construction gives a noble character to this remarkable Norman Romanesque edifice. (Severely damaged; apse destroyed.)

227.-228. SAINT-LO. The *Cathedral of Notre-Dame,* in the town named after the VI century Bishop of Saint Laud, was built during the course of the XIV-XVI centuries. No church had greater charm within its setting, and the towers, built at two different periods, were among the most beautiful in Normandy. (Completely ruined.)

229.-230. CAEN. The *Church of Saint-Gilles,* dating from 1082, rebuilt during the XII and XIII centuries, presents a curious mixture of Gothic and Romanesque elements. The church belonged at one time to the Abbaye aux Dames. (Completely destroyed.)

231. CAEN. The *Escoville Mansion,* one of the supreme examples of French Renaissance civic architecture, was built in 1535–42, by the architect Blaise Le Prestre. It was the house of one Nicolas le Valois, seigneur d'Escoville, about whom little is known beyond the fact that he had suddenly acquired great wealth and that he was interested in alchemy and hermetic philosophy. (Destroyed in large part.)

232.-233. CAEN. The spire of the *Church of Saint-Pierre,* built in 1308, was the prototype of XIV century steeples in Normandy and was generally regarded as the most perfect spire in the region. (Spire destroyed, extensive damage to nave vaulting, but the flamboyant apse is intact.)

234. CAEN. *City Hall,* built in the XVIII century, in the best traditions of French baroque, with a noble restraint in the use of the classical elements. (Destroyed.)

235. CAEN. Fortified portal of the *Castle,* only remains of the extensive fortifications surrounding the castle begun by William the Conqueror and continued by Henry I of England. (Destroyed.)

236. COLLEVILLE-SUR-MER. The square tower of the little church at Colleville-sur-Mer, with its

stone spire, is a rare survival of the XII century. The presence of dormer windows indicates that the architects of Calvados made early use of a device which, in the following century, played an important rôle in the design of church spires. (Completely destroyed.)

237. CAEN. The *"Than" Mansion* (1520–25) displays a mixture of Gothic and Renaissance. In the sculptured pediment of one of the dormer windows can be seen the salamander-dragon motif, which indicates that the house was built in the reign of François I. (Destroyed.)

238. SAINT-PIERRE-SUR-DIVES. One of the two surviving examples of a XIII century public market, within which a remarkable beamed construction supports the slated roof. (Destroyed in part.)

239. BILLY. A XIII century Gothic church, wherein can be noted the exceptional use of a gabled roof on the tower instead of the usual stone spire. (Destroyed.)

240. CARROUGES. XVII century gate-house of an ancient manor house, built in the characteristic style of Normandy. (Entirely gutted, roof destroyed.)

241. NORREY. This XIII century church, a consummate example of the Gothic style in Normandy, with a remarkable sculptured frieze in the ambulatory, was at one time under the control of the Abbey of Saint-Ouen at Rouen. (Vaulting of apse destroyed.)

242. SAINT-SYLVAIN. Small parish church, exemplifying the type of sculptured ornament which persisted in Normandy from as early as the XI century and which likewise became a characteristic style in England. (This church and many others like it in Normandy have been ruined.)

243. COURSEULLES-SUR-MER. *Château.* The style of the dormer windows indicates a building of the early XVII century. (Destroyed.)

244. FALAISE. *Church of Saint-Gervais,* begun in the XI century, with a Norman Romanesque tower and a XIII century nave. (Destroyed in part.)

245. FALAISE. *Trinity Church,* one of the most beautiful structures in Normandy, was built in the course of the XII to XVI centuries, with a flamboyant Gothic apse. (Destroyed in part, including apsidal vaulting.)

246. PONT-L'EVEQUE. *Hôtel Brilly,* an early XVIII century brick and stone mansion. (Destroyed.)

247. PONT-L'EVEQUE. The *"Island" Manor,* or Manoir des Dominicaines de l'Ile, originally part of a Dominican convent, was built in the early XVI century. The half-timbered construction, with deep corbelling, is characteristic of this region. (Destroyed.)

248.-249. LISIEUX. The *"Salamander" House,* an unusual XVI century building, is typical of the Renaissance at Lisieux, and of the decorative principle of accenting the structural members themselves by means of rich carving. (Destroyed.)

250. LISIEUX. *Rue aux Fèvres,* a street which had preserved almost intact its ancient character. Nearly all the houses were half-timbered structures of the XV and XVI centuries. (Largely destroyed.)

251. LISIEUX. *Church of Saint-Jacques* (XV century). Fine example of flamboyant Gothic, possessing complete unity of style, due to the rapidity with which the church was built: 1496–1501. (Almost completely destroyed.)

252.-253. ARGENTAN. *Church of Saint-Germain,* one of the most impressive edifices of the region, built between 1424 and 1641, in the flamboyant Gothic style, with additions in the Renaissance style, notably the towers. (Ruined beyond repair.)

254. CAUDEBEC-EN-CAUX. *House of the Templars* (XIII century), typical Gothic stone house of the period, with two gables facing toward the street. In the interior, the two sections of the house were separated by a row of pillars. (Destroyed.)

255. VIRE. *Church of Notre-Dame,* of the XIII-XV centuries, is built of granite, like most of the buildings in Vire. (Completely gutted, with loss of fine Louis XIV stalls and lobby screens.)

256. ROUEN. No city in France is so rich in masterpieces of mediaeval architecture as Rouen, an episcopal seat since the III century, and since 912 the capital of Normandy, and residence of the dukes. (Although the famous cathedral was seriously damaged, it still stands, as do the churches of St. Maclou and St. Ouen; but completely ruined are many other notable buildings, together with the whole area between the cathedral and the Seine, shown in foreground of plate 256, and the area north and east of the Palais de Justice.)

257. ROUEN. *Cathedral of Notre-Dame* (1270–80). The south nave aisle. (Whole aisle almost completely demolished, including vaulting.)

258. ROUEN. *Cathedral of Notre-Dame.* North transept rose, begun in 1280. (Tracery destroyed.)

259. ROUEN. *Palais de Justice* (Law Courts), begun in 1499, probably by the architects Roger Ango and Rolland Le Roux. The left wing contained the remarkable "Salle des Pas Perdus," or "Salle des Procureurs" (Attorneys' Hall), a large hall with high, timbered vaulting. (The whole building, including the Salle des Pas Perdus, completely ruined.)

260. ROUEN. *Salle des Assises* (Court Room), formerly Parliament Hall, with lavish coffered and gilded oak ceiling with pendentives, dated 1509. (Destroyed.)

261. ROUEN. The *Bourgtheroulde Mansion* (1501–37) was the earliest and most remarkable of the stone mansions at Rouen which subsequently became more common. Guillaume Le Roux, Sieur du Bourgtheroulde, Counsellor of the King, began the building. Le Roux's son, the Abbé d'Aumale, who completed the structure, is noted for having negotiated the treaty between François I and Henry VII of England in their meeting on the "Field of the Cloth of Gold," in 1520. It was due to him, accordingly, that the lower frieze on this façade represents this event in bas-relief. The upper frieze represents scenes from Petrarch's Trionfi. Other sculptural details are stylistically related to the Louis XII château at Blois. (Façade severely damaged.)

262. ROUEN. The so-called *House of Diane de Poitiers* presents the curious anomaly of Gothic construction in wood decorated almost entirely in the Renaissance style. The date of construction is not definitely established, but it must have been prior to 1520, when a city ordinance prohibited overhang and corbelling over streets in Rouen. (Destroyed.)

263. ROUEN. The little Gothic church of *Saint-Vincent*, built in 1511–56, was a flamboyant Gothic edifice almost as elegant as Saint Maclou. It was the setting for the most beautiful stained glass in Rouen, executed by Engrand and Jean Le Prince of Beauvais, ca. 1530. (Church completely demolished, but the glass, having been previously removed, is intact.)

264. ABBEVILLE. The *Church of Saint-Vulfran*, a striking late flamboyant Gothic edifice begun in 1488. The barrel-vaulted choir was, however, not built until the XVII century. (Choir demolished; nave intact. Northwest tower cracked and gutted.)

265. AMIENS. The *"Sagittaire" Mansion*, so-called because the figure of an archer appears at the top of each arch, was built in 1593. By the profusion of decorative elements it can be described as a late provincial interpretation of the Renaissance style. The arches on the ground floor indicate that it was originally intended to be a shop. (Destroyed.)

266. AMIENS. The *Church of Saint-Germain*, an attractive XV century edifice. The sculptures of the portal are of a later date. (Severely damaged throughout.)

267. AMIENS. Originally the *Courthouse of the Royal Bailiff*. Built in 1541, with interesting sculpture on the façade and a remarkable wooden vaulted hall within, it is a very late example of flamboyant Gothic. (Burnt out; façade calcined by fire.)

268. CALAIS. The *Porte de Guise* was all that remained of the Wool Market, built by the English in the early XVI century. It was so called because Henry II of France gave it to Duke François de Guise, liberator of Calais. (Destroyed.)

269. CALAIS. The massive square belfry which adjoins the old *City Hall* was built in the XV century, with an octagonal Renaissance steeple, made of oak covered with lead, added in 1609. (Belfry and City Hall partly demolished.)

270.-271. BEAUVAIS. The area around the cathedral, the old part of Beauvais, although altered through the centuries, still retained the general configuration of its mediaeval past. Particularly notable was the Place de l'Hôtel de Ville, the Place St. Pierre, and various old streets south and east of the cathedral. Notre-Dame-de-la-Basse-Œuvre, a X century structure, the original church which was subsequently replaced by the cathedral, together with houses dating from the XII to the XVII century, were all situated in this area. (Whole area completely leveled. Palais de Justice with round, pointed towers, seen at extreme left, survived.)

272. CASSEL. *Town Hall*, originally the mansion of the Royal Court at Cassel, was rebuilt in the Renaissance style after a fire in 1634. Used as the headquarters of General Foch in 1914-15. (Destroyed.)

273. PONT-A-MOUSSON. On account of its situation between Metz and Toul, the town had a great importance in the Middle Ages, and again later in the XVI century, when the Duke of Lorraine founded a university there. *St. Martin's Church*, belonging originally to the Antonines (Hospital Brothers of St. Anthony), is an important monument of the XV century. (Severely damaged.)

274. TOUL. *City Hall*, formerly the bishop's palace, built in the XVIII century. (Destroyed.)

275.-276. TOUL. *Cathedral of Saint-Etienne*, a masterpiece of flamboyant Gothic. Façade built between 1447 and 1496 by the architects Tristan de Hattonchatel and Jacquemin de Commercy. Nave built in the XIV-XV century; transept and choir, XII century. (The whole cathedral heavily damaged.)

277.-278. SAINT-DIÉ. The interior of the *Cathedral of Saint-Dié* (XII century) shows the exceptional use of Romanesque construction at a time when the Gothic style was already fully developed. Red stone was used in the building. The façade was rebuilt in 1711, after the Thirty Years' War. (Totally destroyed.)

279. STRASBOURG. The *Church of Saint-Etienne*, originally part of a monastery founded in 717, was built about 1172. It was the oldest church edifice in Strasbourg. (Destroyed.)

280. RETHEL. The *Church of Saint-Nicolas* was composed of two churches of different periods joined together. The south portal of the older church shown here is a remarkable example of late Gothic, dated 1510. (Almost totally destroyed.)

281. CHATEAUDUN. The interior of the *Church of the Madeleine* is an excellent example of the sturdy but graceful style which is the special characteristic of XII century ecclesiastical architecture in this region. (Interior ruined.)

282. CHARTRES. *Porte Guillaume*, the only remaining portal of the seven in the ancient fortifications of Chartres, was a fine example of XIV century military architecture. (Almost entirely destroyed.)

283. VERNEUIL. The marvelous spire of the *Madeleine* was erected in the XVI century by the Canon Fillon. It is reminiscent of the Tour de Beurre at Rouen. (Shell-scarred and seriously damaged.)

284. GISORS. The *Church of Saint-Gervais and Saint-Protais* was a vast edifice built during the course of the XII to the XVI century, a factor which gives rise to a curious but interesting mixture of styles. The lower part of the west portal is dated 1537–42, the upper part, 1558–62. (Largely destroyed; west façade ruined.)

285. VENDOME. Since the XV century the *Town Hall* of Vendôme had been established in one of the mediaeval portals of the town, the Porte Saint-Georges. In 1809 the arched vaulting was built in, to allow room for the passage of Napoleon's artillery on the way to Spain. (Building gutted; masonry stands.)

286. NEVERS. The *Cathedral of Saint-Cyr*, an edifice of great importance, was built in various stages from the XI to the XVI century. Its plan, with two apses, one at each end of the church, is of a type associated rather with the Rhenish churches. The north side, shown here, indicates mature flamboyant Gothic construction. (Whole building largely in ruins.)

287. ORLÉANS. *House of Agnes Sorel.* No satisfactory reason can be given why the name of Agnes Sorel, mistress of Charles VII, is associated with this house. It was built in 1529, but the arcade was added subsequently (1540). The capitals are stylistically related to details of the Château de Chambord. (Ruined.)

288. ORLÉANS. *House with Gothic turret* in the flamboyant style of the XV century. The bas-reliefs around the turret represent scenes from the life of the Virgin. (Destroyed.)

289. SAINT-AIGNAN. West wing of the *Château*, a typical example of French Renaissance architecture, built not later than 1535. (Partly destroyed.)

290. SAINT-AIGNAN. *Collegiate Church* of the XII century, an edifice of striking homogeneity in style. (Church and houses badly damaged.)

291. TOURS. The XV century *Mansion of the White Cross* was originally the Town Hall of the borough of Châteauneuf, a suburb of Tours in the Middle Ages. (Destroyed.)

292. TOURS. *Gouin Mansion*, striking example of a Gothic house, built in 1440, remodelled in the Renaissance style around 1510–20. (Partially destroyed.)

293. PERNES-LES-FONTAINES. The mediaeval *Porte Notre-Dame*, to which was added in 1548 a chapel built over the bridge leading to the portal, constitutes an unusual architectural ensemble. (Bridge and chapel ruined; portal still standing.)

294. MARSEILLES. Until 1850, the *Vieux Port* was the only harbor of this proud maritime city, whose history reaches back to 600 B.C. The old houses along this historic water front constituted the essential character of the city. Included amongst them was the Hôtel de Ville, dated 1663–83. (Whole area levelled.)

GERMANY

295. AACHEN. The *City Hall* was built between 1330 and 1370, on the foundations of the ancient palace of Charlemagne. This continuity of use is of deep significance in the development of the prestige and might of the imperial cities. (Largely ruined.)

296. AACHEN. The Octagon, the central part of the *Cathedral*, was built between 790 and 805 as the Palace Chapel of Charlemagne. It was enlarged in 1355 by the addition of the high Gothic choir, in the XV century by the addition of various chapels. Charlemagne was buried here in 814, and most of his successors, down to 1531, were crowned here. (Choir damaged, but restorable.)

297. BRÜHL. *Schloss Brühl* was built between 1725–70 as the residence of the archbishops of Cologne. The original architects were J. C. Schlaun and François Cuvilles. A magnificent staircase was later added by Balthasar Neumann. (Partly destroyed.)

298.-299. NEUSS. The *Church of St. Quirinus,* begun in 1209, is a rich and well-proportioned example of late Romanesque architecture, with a triconchial choir plan characteristic of the lower Rhenish churches. The dome over the east tower was built in the XVIII century to replace an earlier pyramidal roof. (Transept vaulting and apse completely destroyed.)

300.-301. COLOGNE. *St. Gereon,* the main part of which is the unique decagonal nave, built on the foundations of an early Christian martyrium which sheltered the bodies of the 318 martyrs of the Theban legion who, with their captain, St. Gereon, perished here during the persecution of the Christians under Diocletian. The actual church was built in 1219–27, though remnants of the original structure can be recognized in the lower bays in the interior. (Ruined in part.)

302. COLOGNE. *St. Maria im Capitol* was consecrated in 1049 by Leo IX. The beautiful east end of the church was the first great example in the North of the triconchial plan, which influenced strongly the late Romanesque architecture of the Cologne region. The name of the church is reminiscent of the Roman origin of the city. (Entirely destroyed.)

303. COLOGNE. View from the steeple of the cathedral, looking down on the *Church of St. Andrew* (XIII century) and the surrounding houses which, though rebuilt in the XVIII and XIX centuries, yet still suggest, by their arrangement, the original mediaeval setting. (All buildings completely ruined.)

304. COLOGNE. The *Gürzenich,* a name derived from a noble family of Cologne, was built in 1441–47 as a "Herren-Tanzhaus," for official festivities of the city. Good example of stone construction, showing elements of castle building in the battlements and turrets, used here purely as ornament. (Completely destroyed.)

305. COLOGNE. *Gross St. Martin,* built after 1185. A special version of the triconchial plan (cf. # 302) is the building up of the central tower to a great height, accompanied by four slender corner towers. It makes a mighty vertical accent above the roofs of the surrounding houses. (Completely destroyed.)

306. COLOGNE. The exquisite Renaissance *porch of the City Hall,* which was added on to the main structure in 1569–71, from plans by Wilhelm Wernickel. (Destroyed.)

307. COLOGNE. The *City Hall,* viewed from the Old Market Place. This façade dates from about 1550; other parts of the building are older, the tower being erected 1407–14, and the whole built upon the foundations of a Roman stronghold. The tower was built with the proceeds of penalty fees of noble families, after their defeat by the guilds. (Whole building ruined.)

308. COLOGNE. The *City Hall.* The interior of the *Hansa Saal* (ca. 1360), said to be the place where the first general meeting of the Hanseatic League took place on November 19, 1367. The nine figures in the niches represent heroes from Antiquity, Judaism and Christianity, three from each. (Destroyed.)

309. COLOGNE. Interior of the church dedicated to *St. Ursula* (one of the patron saints of Cologne) and her 11,000 companions on the site of an early Christian graveyard. The original XII century construction is apparent in the walls of the nave, while the nave vaulting and the choir show the XIII and XIV century restorations. (Entirely destroyed.)

310. PADERBORN. *City Hall* erected in 1612, in the effective forms of early baroque. The open porches were used for the law courts ("Gerichtslaube") of the city. (Gutted, building a hollow shell.)

311. PADERBORN. *Cathedral.* The mighty western tower, which up to the height of the gables dates from the time of Bishop Meinwerk (1009–36), is a very good example of Westphalian high Romanesque architecture, simple, but as massive as a fortification. The spire is modern. (Extensive fire and shell damage throughout.)

312. MÜNSTER. *Town Hall,* a beautiful example of Gothic civic architecture, built 1335. The horizontal accents of the lower floors are contrasted with the vertical elegance of the gable. The Treaty of Westphalia (1648), after the Thirty Years' War, was signed in this building. (Completely ruined.)

313. MÜNSTER. *Church of St. Ludger,* built about 1200. In spite of later additions (central tower XIII-XV century, choir XV), the church retained some of its original simple Westphalian character. (Total loss, except for façade and central tower.)

314. MÜNSTER. *Cathedral of SS. Peter and Paul*, built in the XIII century as a double choir church. This original disposition was decisively changed when, in 1508–22, the west choir was opened up by the rich Gothic portal and tracery shown here. (Partly destroyed, including west portal.)

315. MÜNSTER. *City Wine House*, built 1615 by Johann von Bocholt, shows beautiful adaptation of the Gothic gable house to Renaissance forms. Building used as an inn as well as for the storing of wine. (Destroyed.)

316. MINDEN. *Cathedral of St. Peter*, built in second half of XIII century, a hall church, i.e., with three naves of equal height, a favorite Westphalian elevation which unites the entire church into one wide open space. An early Gothic edifice of great consequence. (Interior completely ruined; west façade still standing.)

317. XANTEN. The *Collegiate Church of St. Victor*, built 1363–1512, showing the effective combination of stout Romanesque towers, in the typical Rhenish tradition, with a high Gothic nave and façade. An equally interesting Gothic interior made the church altogether one of the most beautiful in the Rhineland. (Destroyed in large part.)

318. OSNABRÜCK. *Cathedral of SS. Peter and Paul*, an impressive example of a widespread tendency in German architecture to accept contrasts of style resulting from different building periods. In this case, the Romanesque left-hand tower is combined with the Gothic forms of the rose window and right-hand tower; both towers in turn surmounted by baroque spires, the whole fused to a living unity. (Partially destroyed.)

319. MAINZ, seat of an archbishopric since the VIII century and one of the seven electorates of the Holy Roman Empire, became a powerful city during the Middle Ages. The *Old Market Place*, shown here, stretches along the north side of the cathedral. The Market Well, at the right, is an outstanding Renaissance work, erected 1526. (Entire area destroyed; cathedral intact except for roof which was burnt.)

320. MAINZ. *St. Peter's Church*, superb and spacious hall church, built in 1748–56 by J. V. Thomann, with fine rococo decoration and ceiling paintings. (Largely ruined; vaulting in part collapsed and stucco decoration damaged beyond repair.)

321. MAINZ. *Electoral Palace*. The corner shown in this plate belongs to the part erected in 1627 by Archbishop Georg von Greiffenklau. This was one of the few good pure Renaissance buildings in Germany. (Destroyed.)

322. COBLENZ. The *Church of St. Castor* was originally founded in 836 by Louis the Pious, successor of Charlemagne. The present structure is an important X century example of a Romanesque double tower façade rebuilt and enlarged in the XII century. (Severely damaged; vaulting of nave destroyed.)

323. TRIER. As one of the earliest Roman settlements in Germany, founded by Augustus, Trier became the most important city of Roman Germany. However, the mediaeval town on the identical site developed along independent lines. The *Market Place*, shown here, is of irregular form, surrounded by houses of the XV to XVII centuries. The "Rotes Haus" at the corner, built ca. 1470, as the festival house of the city, had originally open arcades on the ground floor. (Area devastated.)

324. TRIER. The *Abbey of St. Matthew* is a Benedictine foundation which goes back to early Christian times. The present Abbey Church dates from the XII and the cloisters from the XIII century. (All buildings adjacent to the Abbey devastated, the church itself severely damaged.)

325.-326. TRIER. *Church of Our Lady*, on a masterfully spaced central plan, erected in 1242–53, is a very rare form in Gothic architecture. The rich west portal is a striking example of how harmoniously, in this first great period of Gothic, full-round sculpture is combined with the tectonic elements of the architecture. The whole building is one of the first and finest examples of early Gothic in Germany, introduced from France. (Largely ruined.)

327. TRIER. *Kesselstadt Palace*, built in 1742 by J. V. Thomann for a member of the von Kesselstadt family, a canon of the cathedral. The structure is very skillfully adapted to a curve of the street, lending a characteristically baroque swinging movement to the whole façade. (Destroyed.)

328. CASSEL. The *Orangerie*, built 1701–11, for Landgrave Carl von Hessen, perhaps by the French architect Paul du Ry. Fine example of the elegant summer residences which the princes of that time built near to their main residence for all kinds of intimate court festivals. (In large part destroyed.)

329. GIESSEN. The *Old Schloss*, a structure which had been recently restored to its original XV-XVI century form. (Destroyed.)

330. DARMSTADT. The *Palace of the Grand Duke*, residence of one branch of the Hessian

family, was actually begun in 1375 and rebuilt by Landgrave George I in 1568–95. The section shown is, however, a later addition, built 1716–27 after plans by J. de la Fosse. (Gutted in large part.)

331.-332. DARMSTADT. *Market Place.* The view is taken from a portal of the Grand-Ducal Palace (cf. plate 330), looking toward the mediaeval part of the city, the tower being the belfry of the Gothic Stadtkirche. This section of the town, with narrow, irregular streets, is in sharp contrast to the area around the palace which was built in the XVIII century on a regular plan, with wide, open streets and squares. (Whole city generally ruined.)

333. WORMS. *St. Paul's Church,* showing west façade built up as a transept, in the beautiful, solid Romanesque ashlar characteristic of the Worms tradition. The unusual cupolas of the two small towers are reminiscent of Eastern forms. (Severely damaged.)

334. FRANKFURT-AM-MAIN. The *Römer* (second house from left), named after a family owning the site in the XIV century, was rebuilt as the City Hall in 1405, which was subsequently enlarged by the addition of the adjoining houses. On the ground floor, the Römer consisted of market halls; on the upper floor was the great hall in which the electoral princes served the banquet to the newly elected emperor, both reminders of the two important events which contributed greatly to the celebrity of the city: one, the election of the Roman king and prospective emperor of the Holy Roman Empire, customary since the XII century, legal from 1356 on; the other the great biennial fair, in spring and autumn, at which assembled merchants from every part of Europe. By its wide open space, which was at the same time intimately framed by beautiful houses, the Römerberg constituted one of the outstanding achievements of mediaeval city building. (Whole square completely ruined.)

335. FRANKFURT-AM-MAIN. The *Domplatz,* in the area adjoining the eastern end of the cathedral. To the left, the city weigh house for flour, with the debtors' jail in the upper story. In center, behind, "Haus Fürsteneck," a rare, castle-like stone house, built after 1360. (Completely ruined.)

336. FRANKFURT-AM-MAIN. The *House "Zur Goldenen Waage"* was built in 1628 by a rich merchant, an immigrant from Tournai. Ornate example of a half-timbered house with a ground-floor of stone. In recent years, the house belonged to the Historical Museum and was furnished in the style of the XVII century. (Destroyed.)

337. FRANKFURT-AM-MAIN. *Alter Markt,* the old main street leading from the "Römerberg" to the "Dom" in a smooth curve, solemnly dominated by the tower of the cathedral. Along this way the new king returned to the city hall after the election in the cathedral. Many of the individual houses were quite simple half-timbered structures, but in the aggregate this old section, which had preserved almost unaltered the mediaeval life, was of incomparable charm. (Whole area ruined; cathedral still standing.)

338. FRANKFURT-AM-MAIN. The *Church of Our Lady,* built in the XIV-XV century, was enriched by a beautiful south portal (ca. 1418), with tympanum representing the Adoration of the Kings, a masterpiece of Rhenish sculpture. (Church gutted; south portal severely damaged.)

339. FRANKFURT-AM-MAIN. *City Hall.* Graceful open staircase, in pure Renaissance forms, erected in 1627 for the "Haus Limpburg" which originally belonged to a society of noblemen but later became a part of the City Hall. These open staircases were usually, as here, situated in the courtyard. (Destroyed.)

340.-341. ASCHAFFENBURG. The *Schloss,* beautifully situated on the Main river, was built in 1605–14 by Georg Ridinger. Its square plan with inner courtyard relates it to mediaeval castle architecture but, by its size and unity as well as its style, it is one of the most important monuments of the German Renaissance. (Totally ruined.)

342. MANNHEIM. The *Schloss,* built 1720–60 for the Palsgrave of Bavaria. The plan of this very extensive structure, having a façade 656 yards long, and large "cour d'honneur," is derived from the French château scheme of Hardouin-Mansart. The exterior shows the influence of French classicism; the interior is rich in decoration by Italian, French and German artists. (Gutted and severely damaged throughout.)

343.-344. BRUCHSAL. The *Schloss,* which was the residence of the Prince Bishops of Speyer, was begun in 1720 by Ritter zu Grünstein. Balthasar Neumann built 1731 its famous staircase, decorated together with the Fürstensaal in 1751 by Feichtmeier in the most elegant and fanciful forms of rococo. (Largely ruined.)

345. KARLSRUHE. The *Schloss* was originally the residence of the Margrave Karl Wilhelm of Baden-Durlach, who transferred his residence thence in 1715. The extraordinary fan-shaped plan of the Schloss governs the plan of the entire city which was laid out shortly after 1715. The central tower is the converging point of 32 radiant streets. (Schloss and city largely in ruins.)

346. KARLSRUHE. *Schloss Gottesaue*, built in 1588–99 on the site of an earlier monastery as the country seat of the Margrave of Baden. Rectangular plan with four corner towers and a fifth one serving as staircase. (Completely ruined.)

347. STUTTGART. The *Stiftskirche*, Church of the Holy Cross, a Gothic hall church built in the XIV-XV century on the site of a Romanesque basilica. Viewed from the peaceful Alter Schloss Platz, with a statue of Schiller in the center. (Buildings completely ruined.)

348.-349. STUTTGART. The *Old Palace*, built 1553 for the Duke of Württemberg by Alberlin Tretsch. The general view of the exterior shows the plan disposed as an irregular square, and the simple architectural forms and corner towers still having the effect of a mediaeval castle. The inner court, with its three-storied loggias, betrays Italian influences. (Completely gutted and partly destroyed.)

350. STUTTGART. The *New Palace*, built after 1744, under Duke Karl Eugen. In contrast to the Old Palace, this is a typical baroque structure of the type originating with Versailles. A very harmonious structure, around three sides of a wide open "cour d'honneur," with smoothly rounded corners, and each side of equal length. The Corps de Logis in the center of the main façade is shown here, illustrating the beautiful but restrained use of baroque ornament. (Completely gutted and partly destroyed.)

351. ULM. *Town Hall*, begun in the XIV century, with additions in the XV and XVI centuries, is basically the type of the Gothic gable house. The exterior pulpit on the south side was for official proclamations. (Largely ruined.)

352. ULM. In this view of the *City Hall and old houses adjoining the Cathedral*, a remarkable survival of the crowded condition of the houses common to German towns from the XV century on can be witnessed. The burghers wanted to be protected by the city walls and in most cases not until the XIX century did cities expand beyond these limits. (Area largely destroyed.)

353. ULM. The *Schwörhaus*, built in 1610–12, a public building to be used chiefly as the city law court and for all kinds of legal acts in which a public oath had to be administered. (Gutted and largely ruined.)

354.-355. ULM, formerly one of the most important of the Swabian imperial cities, had preserved almost intact its mediaeval core, which clustered around the cathedral. This view shows the density of the settlement (as also in plate 352) and the consequent devastating effect of bombing raids. Each view, looking down on approximately the same area, was taken from the cathedral, which was fortunately preserved. The large house in the upper right of plate 355 shows the ruined condition of the Town Hall (cf. plate 351).

356. FREIBURG-IM-BREISGAU. The *Basler Hof*. The irregular disposition of the windows lends credence to the fact that this large building is in reality the result of the remodelling of ten small houses, done in 1510–20. The portal and sculpture were added in 1588, when it became the home of the Chapter of the Cathedral of Basle, fleeing from the Reformation. (Largely ruined.)

357.-358. HEILBRONN. *St. Kilian's Church*, dating from the XIII century but decisively enlarged in the XV and XVI. The nave vaulting as shown was built in the XIX century. (Interior ruined; vaulting destroyed.)

359. HEILBRONN. *Market Place and St. Kilian's Church*, the outstanding feature of the latter being its tower. Originally planned as an extremely high Gothic spire, it was completed instead in 1513–29 in northern Renaissance forms, in a quick succession of receding octagons. (All buildings ruined.)

360. HEILBRONN. *Rathaus*. The entire complex represents various structures dating from the XV to XVIII century. The council chamber within is famous for the activities of Götz von Berlichingen, immortalized by Goethe. (Largely destroyed.)

361.-362. WÜRZBURG. The *Residenz*, the palace of the Bishop of Würzburg, built in 1719–44 by the architect Balthasar Neumann, with the collaboration of others. It is without question the most magnificent of all the German baroque palaces. As at Brühl and Bruchsal, an enormous staircase is its outstanding feature, crowned here with the marvelous ceiling decorations by G. B. Tiepolo. A great variety of halls and rooms make up the extraordinary interiors of the palace, the most important of which, including the Stair Hall, the "Weisser Saal," the "Kaisersaal," the "Gartensaal" and the Hofkirche, were miraculously saved. But the remaining interiors are completely ruined by fire and bomb. The *Venetian Room* (plate 361) gives the full charm of early rococo in the light and graceful ornaments of the ceiling combined with the heavier forms of carved woodwork, and of tapestries representing scenes from the Italian comedy, woven in Würzburg by Andreas Pirot.

The *Mirror Room* (plate 362), usually one of the high points of baroque Schlösser, stands out, even in the richness of the Würzburg Residenz, by a most elegant combination of rocaille ornament and paintings, in a sophisticated asymmetry of design. (Both Venetian and Mirror Room destroyed.)

363. WÜRZBURG. The *Marienkapelle and Haus zum Falken,* an interesting group in which the slender Gothic choir of the Marienkapelle (1392) contrasts with one of the richest of Rococo façades, built ca. 1750. (Chapel gutted; house completely ruined.)

364. WÜRZBURG. *Marienkapelle,* the west façade. The chapel was built about 1377, on the site of a synagogue which was changed into a church during the persecution of the Jews in 1348. (Gutted; tower intact.)

365. WÜRZBURG. The *Old University,* built 1582–91, under Bishop Julius Echter, consists in plan of a square enclosing an inner court. The arcade on the ground floor was originally open, but closed later to install the library. (Gutted; exterior walls standing.)

366. WÜRZBURG. *Stift Haug,* built 1670–71 by Antonio Petrini. While the plan is influenced by Il Gesù in Rome, the façade is rather more representative of the Renaissance, with its surfaces remaining in one plane, and divided into three stories by heavy horizontal mouldings. (Severely damaged, vaulting ruined.)

367. WÜRZBURG. *Neumünster,* formerly a Romanesque basilica which was remodelled and enlarged in 1711 and succeeding years. In contrast to Stift Haug (plate 366), this is a very good example of the baroque façades of southern Germany, with its swinging movement and concentration of accent toward the center. (Edifice gutted, exterior shell-scarred and generally damaged.)

368. BAMBERG. *Town Hall.* Formerly a Gothic bridge tower standing on an island in the Pegnitz river, the originally austere, military character of the structure was skillfully transformed in 1744–56 into the peacefully inviting baroque of this graceful Town Hall, a masterpiece of civic architecture. (Whole structure severely damaged by the demolition of the nearby bridge.)

369. ROTHENBURG. The *Weisser Turm* belongs to the inner fortification ring of the city. Built in the XII–XIII century, it exemplifies the extremely solid masonry and elemental forms of Romanesque fortifications, especially effective in the setting of the narrow street. The two upper stories and the spire rebuilt in the XVIII century. (Upper part of

tower and all the houses ruined; lower part of tower still stands.)

370. ROTHENBURG. *View* taken from the Town Hall, looking eastward. The unique value of the whole city as a monument of mediaeval city-building is well demonstrated by this view, revealing its organic growth through the centuries by the irregular combination of small open squares and narrow winding streets. In the upper extreme left appears the Weisser Turm of the inner XII–XIII century fortifications, and farther off, the Würzburger Tor of the exterior wall, dating from the XIV–XV century.

371. ROTHENBURG. View of a *destroyed area,* seen from the Town Hall. In general, the eastern part of the town between the Würzburg Gate and the Röder Gate, and the center of the town are completely ruined by fire and explosives.

372. NÜREMBERG. The fame of Nüremberg rests on having been one of the great mediaeval cities of Europe. Growing from the XI century on, around two cores, an imperial farm and an imperial castle, it had in 1400 about 20,000 inhabitants, rivalling Cologne in the west. In the XVI century it was an outstanding center of crafts and trade, of art and general cultural achievement. This *view,* taken from the castle, comprises St. Sebald and the surrounding area in the immediate foreground, and St. Lorenz in the distance, where originally the imperial farm was located, the two cores or nuclei of development referred to above.

373. NÜREMBERG. The destruction of the mediaeval part is complete. Only the larger churches of St. Sebald and St. Lorenz still stand. In the immediate foreground lower left may be identified the Heilige Geist Hospital (plate 379), while at the top left, partly out of picture, is St. Lorenz, with its roof gone.

374. NÜREMBERG. *Houses on the Pegnitz River,* showing in center the Wasserturm (XIII–XV century), to the left the Weinstadel, or storehouse for wine. Immediately behind the Wasserturm appear the steeples of St. Sebald and, at extreme left background, the castle. (Whole complex completely ruined.)

375. NÜREMBERG. *Peller Haus,* built in 1605 for the merchant Martin Peller by Jacob Wolff the Elder. Showing influences from both Venice and Flanders, it is basically a very rich example of the German late Renaissance. (Destroyed.)

376. NÜREMBERG. *Frauenkirche,* dedicated in 1355 by Emperor Charles IV, on the site of the old synagogue destroyed in the riots of 1348. A hall

church on a square ground plan, it has a remarkable façade with a protruding porch surmounted by a little chapel. (Completely ruined.)

377. NÜREMBERG. The *Market Place*, looking toward the northwest corner, in the direction of St. Sebald. (All buildings completely ruined, except for the "Schöne Brunnen" in center, which was saved by protective masonry.)

378. NÜREMBERG. The *Fleisch-Brücke*, one of the bridges across the Pegnitz, connecting the two original sections out of which the city grew (cf. plate 372). Built 1596–98 by Jacob Wolff the Elder, with a design based on the Rialto Bridge in Venice. (Area in ruins.)

379. NÜREMBERG. *Holy Ghost Hospital*, built 1341, enlarged 1488–1527. This view shows the courtyard with open wooden galleries, which was changed in the XVII or XVIII century from a closed, two-aisle Gothic hall. The Holy Ghost Hospitals, instituted in many cities, were foundations of the citizens, in contrast to those founded by monastic orders. (Destroyed.)

380. MUNICH. The *Marienplatz*, the market place of Old Munich, at the end of which stands the old Town Hall (built 1315, rebuilt 1470) with its graceful spire. In the foreground, the Mariensäule, typical monument of many Bavarian and Austrian towns. (Old Town Hall and surrounding structures largely in ruins.)

381. MUNICH. *Frauenkirche*, founded in 1271, rebuilt 1468–88 by Jörg Ganghofer, a triple-nave hall church of soaring proportions. On the exterior, the towers with their famous copper-green cupolas are a familiar landmark. (Choir and nave heavily damaged; vaulting of choir partly broken. Towers intact.)

382. MUNICH. The *Residenz*, palace of the dukes of Bavaria, is a vast complex, built from the XVI to the XVIII century. The *Antiquarium*, built in 1560 as the "Kunst und Wunderkammer" of Duke Albrecht V, was one of the earliest museum halls in existence. (Ruined.)

383. MUNICH. *Residenz.* A special charm of the Munich Residenz were its interior courtyards. The *Grottenhof*, built in 1580 by Friedrich Sustris, still preserved its original fine and clear Renaissance character in spite of later changes. (Largely ruined.)

384. MUNICH. *Preysing Palace*, ostentatious private residence of the wealthy Bavarian family of von Preysing, built 1720–25 by the architect Joseph Effner. (Largely ruined.)

385. MUNICH. The *Church of the Theatines*, or St. Cajetans Hofkirche, built in 1663–75. According to the special wishes of the Prince Elector Ferdinand Maria, the design was based on the church of Sant'Andrea della Valle, but enriched by the use of the double towers, a northern conception. The Feldherrn Halle appears to the left. (Damage to the church general and heavy. Interior largely ruined by fire.)

386. A. & B. MUNICH. *St. Anna Damen Stiftskirche*, built in 1732–35, was decorated on the interior by the famous brothers Asam, and is one of the principal works of high baroque in Munich. The comparatively simple exterior leads into a harmonious unity of space, light, and decorative elements which still retains a tectonic strength, a quality soon lost in the pictorial tendency of German rococo. (Completely destroyed.)

387. MUNICH. *St. Michaels Hofkirche*, erected 1583–88 by Duke Wilhelm V for the Jesuits. A most important work of the early baroque in Germany, derived from but not a copy of Il Gesù in Rome, and itself a model for many later works. By eliminating the cupola at the crossing, the mighty barrel vault gains absolute dominance, uniting the entire interior in one great accent. (Vaulting destroyed.)

388. AUGSBURG. In the *Town Hall*, the Golden Hall, named on account of its gilded Renaissance ornamentation, was one of the most superb interiors of its kind in Germany. Its chief importance was in its monumental size, not only in length and width, but more particularly in its great height, running through three stories, which was unique in the north, and made it very harmonious in proportions. (Destroyed by fire.)

389.-390. AUGSBURG, of Roman origin, an important art and commercial center in the Middle Ages, trading with the north as well as with Italy and the Near East, reached the height of its prosperity in the XV and XVI centuries. In this view of the *Karolinen Strasse* can be seen at the left the imposing City Hall and the adjacent slender Perlach Tower, originally a watch tower. Both the City Hall and a reconstruction of the Perlach Tower were carried out by Elias Holl in the early XVII century. (Plate 390 shows present condition.)

391. AUGSBURG. The *Fugger House*, built in 1512–15 for Jacob Fugger, outstanding member of the family of merchant princes who accumulated so large a fortune that they became not only a decisive factor in the development of European capitalism, but known also for their munificence in the sponsorship of the arts and humanistic endeavors. The Fugger House, situated on the broad Maximilianstrasse, was in ground plan basically derived from Italian palaces, with inner courtyards; but with its long sloping roof it is well adapted to its surroundings. (Completely gutted and in part demolished.)

392.-393. ESSLINGEN. The *Town Hall,* a simple but extremely sturdy half-timbered structure of the XV century. This was enriched in 1589 by a Renaissance façade, facing on the market place (plate 392). The rear view (plate 393) shows the original structure. (Completely destroyed.)

394. HILDESHEIM. The *Kaiserhaus,* built in 1586 for the lawyer Caspar Borkholt. So called on account of the medallions of 44 emperors carved in the stone foundation at street level. The carved ornament, which was intended to cover the whole façade, was never completed. Rare example of stone architecture in a city of prevailing wood construction. (Destroyed.)

395.-396. HILDESHEIM. The *Knochenhauer Amtshaus* was built in 1529 as the guildhouse of the Butchers' Guild, the most powerful of all by its wealth. Even in a region where beautiful half-timbered houses are abundant, this one was outstanding. It was as perfect in construction as in form, a climax in the development of an indigenous style evolved originally from the Germanic peasant house. (Completely destroyed.)

397. HILDESHEIM. *St. Michael's Church,* built 1001–33 under the personal supervision of Bishop Bernward, who was specially versed in arts and crafts. Having originally a western entrance, adorned with the famous bronze doors, it was changed (ca. 1033) into a double choir church to shelter Bernward's tomb in the western crypt. The most important monument of early Romanesque in Germany, with perfect proportions in plan and elevation. The pure tectonic forms were enriched in 1186 by High Romanesque capitals, a richly sculptured choir screen, and a painted ceiling representing the Tree of Jesse. (Gutted and partly ruined.)

398. HILDESHEIM. *St. Andrew's Church,* originally Romanesque, was rebuilt and enlarged in the XV-XVI century. The Gothic west tower and spire dates from the early XVI century. In left foreground, one of the beautiful half-timbered houses adorned with rich carvings for which Hildesheim was famous. (Church largely ruined, houses destroyed.)

399. BRUNSWICK was founded in the XI century,

became famous in the XII as the residence of Duke Henry the Lion of the Wolf family. The *Old Town Hall,* with two wings at right angles, occupies one corner of the wide market place. Originally a rather simple gabled structure, it was enriched about 1400 by the addition of the Gothic arcade with elaborate open tracery in the upper story. (Building gutted and partly ruined.)

400. BRUNSWICK. The *Old House,* dated 1536, is a very good example of the famous half-timbered houses of Brunswick, standing always with their broad sides facing toward the street (i.e., gable ends at a right angle to the street), resulting in monumental façades. The structural timber work was accented with rich carvings. In this house, the plain section in the lower right is a later alteration. (Ruined by fire, as many others in Brunswick.)

401. DRESDEN, the residence of the prince elector of Saxony, became a celebrated center of baroque architecture during the XVIII century under the reign of August the Strong, king of Poland. The *Schloss* (at right), built in successive stages from the XV century on, was connected around 1740 with the newly built Catholic Hofkirche (left) by this elegant bridge, for the private use of the princely family. (Whole complex largely destroyed.)

402. DRESDEN. The Catholic *Hofkirche,* built in 1738–46 by a Roman architect, Gaetano Chiaveri. In spite of many Roman baroque influences in detail forms, the general scheme, with dominating western front tower, is decisively German in character, which results in a rare harmony of northern and southern idioms. (Largely ruined.)

403.-404. DRESDEN. The *Zwinger,* built in 1711–22 by Daniel Pöpelmann as a race course and festival place for the princely court. Consisting of an open courtyard surrounded by buildings of one or two stories for the spectators, it combines strong and fine architecture with very rich sculptural ornament. (Largely ruined.)

405.-406. DRESDEN. *Frauenkirche,* built in 1726–38 by Georg Bähr. The most important example of Protestant ecclesiastical architecture in the XVIII century. The oval dome, with its high lantern, has the strength of a central tower, concentrating and uplifting the whole structure in one soaring accent. (Completely destroyed.)

407. LÜBECK. *Town Hall Square and Marienkirche.* The city, founded in 1143, came into the possession of Henry the Lion in 1159. After Henry's death Frederic Barbarossa made it a free city. By its position of leadership in the Hanseatic League during the XIII and XIV centuries, its importance became paramount. From this time date the *Town Hall* and the *Marienkirche,* both outstanding monuments, expressive of the wealth, the pride, and the cultural ambitions of the "Bürger" as a new social class. (Largely ruined.)

408. LÜBECK. The *Marienkirche,* built in the second half of the XIII century as the principal parish church of the city, is a Gothic basilica showing in its choir plan influences from Bruges or Tournai. It is the most perfect example of brick architecture, and was the prototype of almost all the churches in the Baltic region. Evidence of the sumptuousness of the interior appointments can be gained from this view of the south side of the nave. The richly carved pew is the "Bürgermeisterstuhl," destined for the mayors; it was made in 1574–75 by Joachim Wernke the Elder. (Largely ruined; vaulting destroyed.)

409. LÜBECK. *Town Hall,* showing the northern wing of the market place façade. The towering wall surmounted by pinnacles, built end of XIII century, enlarged in the XV, serves to both unite and conceal older sections behind the wall, consisting of two separate houses dating from the first half of the XIII century. To the mighty character of this pinnacled structure is added the more elegant Renaissance building in front, dating from 1570. (Largely ruined.)

410. LÜBECK. *Town Hall,* showing a section of the eastern wing along the "Breitestrasse," built in the XIV-XV century. In the windows above can be seen the very skillful use of bricks for architectural ornament. The picturesque external staircase was added in 1594. (Largely ruined.)

411. LÜBECK. The *Salt Houses,* dating from the XIV century, were used for the storage of salted herring, one of the products which played a large part in the early prosperity of Lübeck. (Destroyed.)

412. EMDEN. The *Rathaus,* built 1574–76 by Laurens van Steenwinkel of Antwerp, was to some degree modelled on the Antwerp City Hall. The forms however of the Emden Town Hall are simpler, yet very effective, with good proportions. The tower was placed off center in the building undoubtedly in order to form an axis with the bridge facing it. (Completely gutted.)

413. HAMBURG. *Canal off the Binnenhafen.* Hamburg was one of the great Hanseatic cities, ultimately to become the most important port of Germany. In the area around the Binnenhafen, or Binnen-Alster, an old inner basin of the port, the old city is crossed by several narrow canals, called "flet," connecting the Alster with the Elbe. These canals are bordered by huge warehouses. (Area partly ruined.)

414. KÖNIGSBERG. The *Schloss,* built in 1257 as a castle of the Order of the Teutonic Knights. After the fall of Marienburg in the XV century, it became the seat of the Grand Masters of the order. Changes and additions to the Schloss in the XVI and XVIII centuries considerably enlarged the original structure, to which period belong the round tower, or bastion. (Largely ruined.)

415. BERLIN. *Charlottenburg Schloss* erected in 1695–99 as the summer residence of Sophie Charlotte, wife of the Prince Elector Frederick III. The architect was A. Nering. It was enlarged in 1701 by Eosander von Göthe. An unusual feature of baroque schloss architecture is the high cupola tower, completed in 1711 with a crowning figure of Fortuna. (Ruined.)

416.-417. BERLIN. The *Französische Kirche,* together with the identical Neue Kirche, was begun in 1701 on the Gendarmen-Markt. In 1780–85, under Frederick the Great, to each church was added a high cupola tower by Unger, after plans by Gontard. These impressive superstructures, together with the temple façades of the lower pedimented structures, constituted outstanding monuments of classicism in Berlin. (Largely ruined.)

418. BERLIN. The *Schloss,* originally the residence of the electors of Brandenburg, but after 1701 that of the Prussian kings, was begun in 1443. The building got its real importance when in 1698, the Prince Elector Frederick III (later King Frederick I of Prussia) gave the order to Andreas Schlüter for a new building. The most important part of Schlüter's building is the inner court (plate 418), showing the mighty forms of Roman baroque. After 1706, the Schloss was completed by Eosander von Göthe. (Largely ruined.)

419. BERLIN. *Monbijou,* near Spandauer Tor, was built in 1706 for the Countess von Wartenburg by Eosander von Göthe. The interior, with subsequent alterations, shows less vigorous and fanciful rococo forms than were developed in Franconia and Bavaria, more in the somewhat restricted idiom of authentic French taste. More recently, the building sheltered the Hohenzollern Museum. (Destroyed.)

AUSTRIA

420. VIENNA. The upper *Belvedere* was built in 1721–23 as summer palace for Prince Eugen, by Lukas von Hildebrandt. Born in Genoa, Hildebrandt was naturally greatly influenced by the great Italian baroque, but at the same time he developed his own strong and joyful style, with abundant use of sculpture. (Right wing destroyed.)

421.-422. VIENNA. *Stephansdom,* begun in 1304, was largely built during the XIV and XV centuries. The south spire, together with the mighty sloping roof, a beloved landmark of Vienna and all Austria, was completed in 1433. The interior, built in the form of a hall church, is a very fine example of the rich pictorial style of late Gothic. Plate 422 shows the star vaulting with hanging keystone of the St. Barbara chapel, adjoining the north transept, and completed in 1476. Surrounding the Dom is one of the oldest sections of Vienna. (Dom seriously damaged. Roof completely destroyed; vaulting of apse partly destroyed. Adjacent houses partly destroyed.)

423. VIENNA. *Kinsky Palace,* built in 1709–13 for Count Wierich Philip Daun by Lukas von Hildebrandt. Perfect in proportions, together with a harmonious balance of architecture and ornament, this façade ranks very high in the great number of excellent works of this period. (Largely ruined.)

HUNGARY

424.-427. BUDAPEST. The *Royal Palace* originated with a castle built by King Bela IV in 1247. It was enlarged by Sigismund, and especially by Matthias Corvinus, 1458–90. In the period of the Turkish War it still existed as a fortress. Empress Maria Theresa started a new building after the plans of Lukas von Hildebrandt, carried out partly in 1769. This new building was enlarged 1894–1906, which resulted in a façade a thousand feet wide, very impressively situated above the Danube. The Széchenyi Bridge was built by the English engineer William Tierney Clark in 1842; it was the oldest of the bridges in Budapest. (Royal Palace and all bridges completely destroyed. Budapest in general is one of the most completely ruined cities of central Europe.)

1. Danzig: City Hall (XIV–XVI century)
   Dantzig: L'Hôtel de Ville (XIVe–XVIe siècle)

2. Danzig: Arsenal (XVII century)
Danzig: L'Arsenal (XVIIe siècle)

3. Danzig: St. Mary's Church (xiv century) and the City
Dantzig: Eglise Sainte-Marie (xive siècle) et la Ville

4. Danzig: Old Water Front
   Dantzig: Vieux Quai

5. Danzig: Warehouses (XIV century)
   Dantzig: Entrepôts (XIVe siècle)

6. Warsaw: Old Market Square (XIV–XVIII century)
   Varsovie: Vieux Marché (XIVe–XVIIIe siècle)

7. Warsaw: St. John's Cathedral. Façade
Varsovie: Cathédrale Saint-Jean. Façade

Warsaw: St. John's Cathedral (XIV century)
Varsovie: Cathédrale Saint-Jean (XIVe siècle)

9. Warsaw: Old Market Square
   Varsovie: Vieux Marché

10. Warsaw: Old Market Square in Ruins
    Varsovie: Vieux Marché en Ruines

11. Warsaw: Fukier House (XVIII century)
Varsovie: Hôtel Fukier (XVIIIe siècle)

12. Warsaw: Lazienski Palace (XVIII century)
Varsovie: Palais Lazienski (XVIIIe siècle)

13. Warsaw: Lazienski Palace. Hall of Solomon
Varsovie: Palais Lazienski. Salle de Salomon

14. Warsaw: Krasiński Palace (XVII century)
Varsovie: Palais Krasinski (XVIIe siècle)

15. Warsaw: Castle Square
Varsovie: Place du Château

16. Warsaw: Royal Castle. Hall of Audiences (XVIII century)
    Varsovie: Château Royal. Salle de Réception (XVIIIe siècle)

17. Warsaw: Royal Castle. Ballroom (XVIII century)
    Varsovie: Château Royal. Salle de Bal (XVIIIe siècle)

18. Warsaw: Staszic Palace (XIX century)
Varsovie: Palais Staszic (XIXe siècle)

20. Warsaw: Church of the Holy Virgin (xv century)
    Varsovie: Eglise de la Sainte Vierge (xve siècle)

19. Warsaw: St. Anne's Church (xv–xviii century)
    Varsovie: Eglise Sainte-Anne (xve–xviiie siècle)

21. Płock: Cathedral (XII century)
Płock: La Cathédrale (XIIIe siècle)

22. Lwow: Church of the Bernardine Monks (XVII century)
Lwow: Eglise des Bernardins (XVIIe siècle)

23. Poznan: Cathedral (XIV–XVIII century) and Church of the Holy Virgin
Poznan: La Cathédrale (XIVe–XVIIIe siècle) et Eglise de la Sainte Vierge

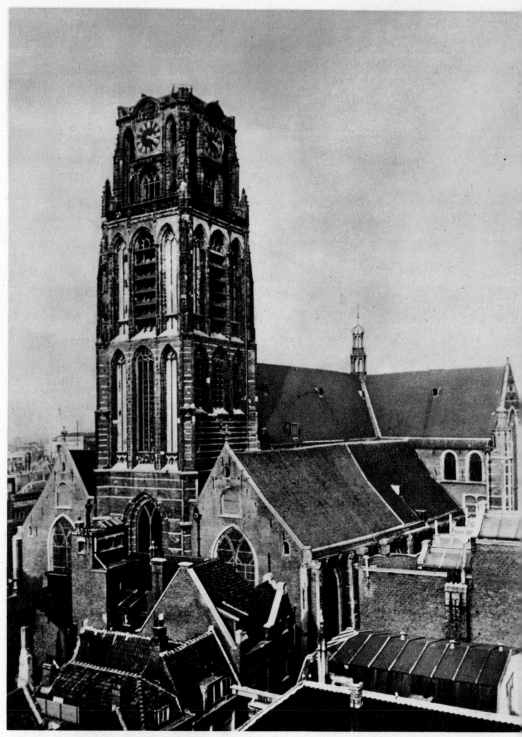

24. Rotterdam: Church of St. Lawrence (xv century)
    Rotterdam: Eglise Saint-Laurent (xve siècle)

Rotterdam: Ruins of Church of St. Laurence and the Steiger Canal
Rotterdam: Eglise Saint-Laurent et Canal Steiger en Ruines

26. Rotterdam: Church of St. Laurence. Apse
Rotterdam: Eglise Saint-Laurent. Abside

27. Rotterdam: The Steiger Canal
    Rotterdam: Canal Steiger

28. Heusden: Town Hall
   Heusden: L'Hôtel de Ville

29. Middelburg: Military Hospital (xvii century)
Middelbourg: Hôpital Militaire (xviiᵉ siècle)

30. Middelburg: Former Abbey of the Premonstratensians (XII–XVII century)
Middelbourg: Ancienne Abbaye des Prémontrés (XIIe–XVIIe siècle)

31. Middelburg: Town Hall (xv century)
Middelbourg: L'Hôtel de Ville (xve siècle)

32. Middelburg: The "Steenrots" House (1590)
Middelbourg: Hôtel "Steenrots" (1590)

33. Sluis: Town Hall (XIV century)
Sluis: L'Hôtel de Ville (XIVe siècle)

34. Arnhem: Market Place
Arnhem: Le Grand Marché

35. Arnhem: St. Eusebius' Church (xv century)
Arnhem: Eglise Saint-Eusèbe (xve siècle)

36. Venlo: St. Martin's Church (XIII–XV century)
Venlo: Eglise Saint-Martin (XIIIe–XVe siècle)

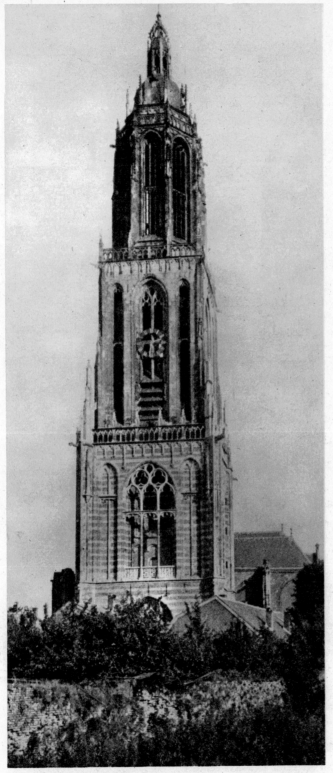

37. Rhenen: Spire of the Church of St. Cunera (xv century)
Rhenen: Flèche de l'Eglise Sainte-Cunera (xve siècle)

38. Oirschot: Church of St. Peter (XV–XVI century)
Oirschot: Eglise Saint-Pierre (XVe–XVIe siècle)

39. Oirschot: Church of St. Peter. Choir Stalls (XVI century)
   Oirschot: Eglise Saint-Pierre. Stalles du Chœur (XVIe siècle)

40. Wouw: Church of St. Lambert (XVI century)
Wouw: Eglise Saint-Lambert (XVIe siècle)

41. Wouw: Church of St. Lambert. Choir Stalls (XVI century)
Wouw: Eglise Saint-Lambert. Stalles du Chœur (XVIe siècle)

42. Nymegen: Town Hall (1554)
    Nimègue: L'Hôtel de Ville (1554)

Nymegen: Weigh House (1612)
Nimègue: Poids Public (1612)

44. Nymegen: Church of St. Stephen (XIII–XV century)
   Nimègue: Eglise Saint-Etienne (XIIIe–XVe siècle)

45. Nymegen: City Gate (1605)
    Nimègue: Porte de Ville (1605)

46. Hoogstraten: Church of St. Catherine (XVI century)
Hoogstraten: Eglise Sainte-Catherine (XVIe siècle)

47. Hoogstraten: Church of St. Catherine (XVI century)
Hoogstraten: Eglise Sainte-Catherine (XVIe siècle)

48. Hoogstraten: Town Hall (XVI century)
Hoogstraten: L'Hôtel de Ville (XVIᵉ siècle)

49. Nivelles: Church of St. Gertrude. The Cloister (XI century)
Nivelles: Eglise Sainte-Gertrude. Le Cloître (XIe siècle)

51. Bocholt: Parish Church. Altarpiece (XVI century)
Bocholt: Eglise Paroissiale. Retable (XVIe siècle)

50. Nivelles: Reliquary of St. Gertrude (XIII century)
Nivelles: Reliquaire de Sainte Gertrude (XIIIe siècle)

52. Aerschot: Beguine Convent
Aerschot: Béguinage

53. Louvain: Abbey of St. Gertrude. Choir Stalls
Louvain: L'Abbaye de Sainte Gertrude. Stalles du Chœur

54. Bastogne: Church of St. Peter (XII–XVI century)
Bastogne: Eglise Saint-Pierre (XIIe–XVIe siècle)

55. Tournai: General view
Tournai: Vue Générale

56. Tournai: Ruined Section around the Cathedral
Tournai: Quartier détruit autour de la Cathédrale

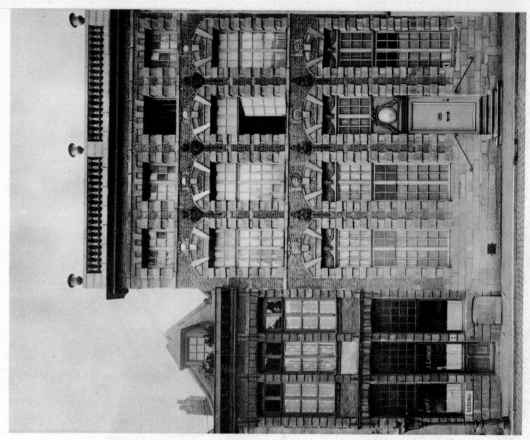

58. Tournai: A xviith century House

57. Tournai: The "Maisons Romaines" (xii century)

59. Tournai: Church of St. Brice (XII century)
Tournai: Eglise Saint-Brice (XIIe siècle)

60. Novgorod: "Granovity" Palace (xv century).
Novgorod: Palais "Granovity" (xve siècle).

61. Novgorod: The Kremlin Walls (xv–xvi century)
Novgorod: Les Murs du Kremlin (xve–xvie siècle)

62. Novgorod: Spas Nereditsky Church (XII century)
Novgorod: Eglise de Spas Nereditsky (XIIe siècle)

63 AND 64. Novgorod: Spas Nereditsky Church. Mural Paintings (XII century)
Novgorod: Eglise de Spas Nereditsky. Peintures Murales (XIIe siècle)

65 AND 66. Novgorod: Spas Nereditsky Church. Mural Paintings (XII century)
Novgorod: Eglise de Spas Nereditsky. Peintures Murales (XIIe siècle)

67. Pskov: Pogankiny Mansion (XVII century)
Pskov: Hôtel Pogankiny (XVIIᵉ siècle)

68. Istra: New Jerusalem Monastery. Dome
Istra: Dôme du Monastère de la Nouvelle Jérusalem

69. Istra: New Jerusalem Monastery (XVII–XVIII century)
    Istra: Monastère de la Nouvelle Jérusalem (XVIIe–XVIIIe siècle)

70. Istra: Ruins of the New Jerusalem Monastery
    Istra: Monastère de la Nouvelle Jérusalem en Ruines

71. Volokolamsk: The Monastery (XVI century)
Volokolamsk: Le Monastère (XVIe siècle)

72. Peterhof: Palace of Peter the Great (xviii century)
Peterhof: Palais de Pierre le Grand (xviiie siècle)

73. Peterhof: Palace of Peter the Great. Garden Pavilion (XVIII century)
Peterhof: Palais de Pierre le Grand. Pavillon (XVIIIe siècle)

Dyetskoye-Selo: Palace of Catherine the Great (XVIII century)
Dyetskoye-Selo: Palais de la Grande Catherine (XVIIIᵉ siècle)

75. Dyetskove-Selo: Palace of Catherine the Great (XVIII century)

76. Dyetskoye-Selo: Palace of Catherine the Great (XVIII century)
Dyetskoye-Selo: Palais de la Grande Catherine (XVIIIe siècle)

77. Dyetskoye-Selo: Alexander Palace (XIX century)
Dyertskoye Selo: Palais d'Alexandre (XIXe siècle)

78. Leningrad: Winter Palace and Admiralty
Leningrad: Palais d'Hiver et l'Amirauté

79. Novgorod Yuriev Monastery. The Cathedral (1119)
Novgorod: Monastère Yuriev. La Cathédrale (1119)

0. Chernigov: Spaso-Preobrazhensk Cathedral (XI century)
Chernigov: La Cathédrale Spaso-Preobrazhensk (XIe siècle)

81. Kiev: Pechersk Lavra (Monastery founded in XI century)
Kiev: Petchersk Lavra (Monastère fondé au XIe siècle)

82. Kiev: Pechersk Lavra (Monastery founded in XI century)
Kiev: Petchersk Lavra (Monastère fondé au XIe siècle)

83. Kiev: Ruins of the Pechersk Lavra
Kiev: Petchersk Lavra en Ruines

84. Canterbury: Cathedral Precincts
Cantorbéry: Maisons dans l'Enceinte de la Cathédrale

85. Plymouth: St. Andrew's Church (XV century)
Plymouth: Eglise Saint-André (XVe siècle)

86 Exeter: Old Houses in High Street (XVI century)
Exeter: Vieilles Maisons de High Street (XVIᵉ siècle)

87. Exeter: Cathedral. Choir (XIII-XIV century)
Exeter: La Cathédrale. Chœur (XIIIᵉ–XIVᵉ siècle)

89. London: All Hallows Church (XIII-XV century)
Londres: Eglise de la Toussaint (XIIIe-XVe siècle)

88. London: Chelsea Old Church (XVII century)
Londres: Eglise de Chelsea (XVIIe siècle)

90. London: All Hallows Church (XIII-XV century)
Londres: Eglise de la Toussaint (XIIIe-XVe siècle)

91. London: St. Bride's (XVII century)
Londres: Eglise Saint-Bride (XVIIe siècle)

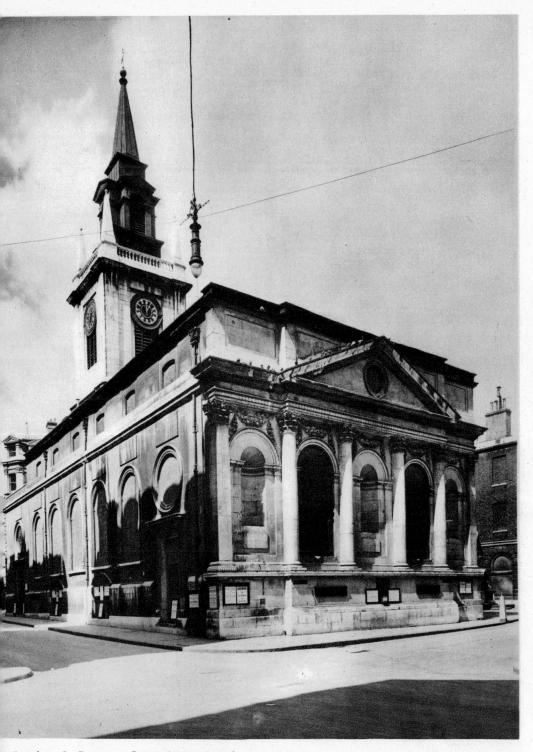

London: St. Lawrence Jewry (XVII century)
Londres: Eglise Saint-Laurent dans l'Ancien Quartier Juif (XVIIe siècle)

93. London: Guild Hall (xv-xviii century)
Londres: Le ''Guild Hall'' (xve-xviiie siècle)

London: Austin Friars' Church (XIV-XIX century)
Londres: Eglise des Augustins (XIVe-XIXe siècle)

London: Middle Temple Hall (XVI century)
Londres: Grande Salle du "Middle Temple" (XVIe siècle)

96. London: Inns of Court. Gray's Inn (XVII century)
Londres: Les Ecoles de Droit. Collège Gray (XVIIe siècle)

98. London: Temple Church (XII-XIX century)
Londres: Eglise des Templiers (XIIIe-XIXe siècle)

97 London: Inns of Court. Pump Court (XVII century)
Londres: Les Ecoles de Droit. Cour de la Pompe (XVIIe siècle)

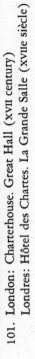

101. London: Charterhouse. Great Hall (XVII century)
Londres: Hôtel des Chartes. La Grande Salle (XVIIe siècle)

100. London: Portman House (XVIII century)
Londres: Hôtel Portman (XVIIIe siècle)

102. Bath: Royal Crescent (XVIII century)
Bath: "Royal Crescent" (XVIIIe siècle)

103. Bristol: Berkeley Square (XVIII century)
Bristol: Place Berkeley (XVIIIe siècle)

104. Bristol: St. Peter's Hospital (xv-xvii century)
Bristol: L'Hospice Saint-Pierre (xve-xviie siècle)

105. Bristol: Church of St. Mary-Le-Port (xv century)
Bristol: Eglise Sainte-Marie-Le-Port (xve siècle)

106. Eton: Upper School (1689)
Eton: L'Ecole Supérieure (1689)

107. Norwich: Cathedral. The Close
Norwich: Maisons dans l'Enclos de la Cathédrale

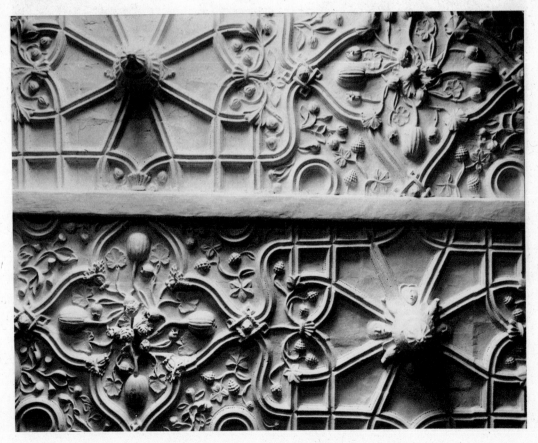

108. Great Yarmouth: Grey Friars' Cloister. Detail of Ceiling (XVI century)
Great Yarmouth: Cloître des Frères Gris. Plafond: Détail (XVIe siècle)

109. Coventry: Ford's Hospital (XVI century)
Coventry: L'Hospice Ford (XVIe siècle)

110. Coventry: St. Michael's Cathedral. Apse (XIV-XV century)
Coventry: La Cathédrale Saint-Michel. Abside (XIVe-XVe siècle)

111. Coventry: Old Quarter adjoining Cathedral
Coventry: Vieux Quartier près de la Cathédrale

112. Manchester: Cathedral (xv century)
Manchester: La Cathédrale (xve siècle)

113. Palermo: San Francesco. Portal (1302)
     Palerme: San Francesco. Portail (1302)

4. Palermo: San Francesco (XIII century)
   Palerme: San Francesco (XIIIe siècle)

115. Benevento: Cathedral (XII century)
    Bénévent: La Cathédrale (XIIe siècle)

. Benevento: Ruins of the Cathedral
Bénévent:　La Cathédrale en Ruines

117. Benevento: Cathedral. Portal (XI-XII century)
Bénévent: La Cathédrale. Portail (XIe-XIIe siècle)

Benevento: Cathedral. Bronze Doors (detail)
Bénévent: La Cathédrale. Portail en Bronze (détail)

119. Benevento: Cathedral (XII-XVII century)
Bénévent: La Cathédrale (XIIe-XVIIe siècle)

120. Benevento: Cathedral. Pulpit
Bénévent: La Cathédrale. Chaire

121. Naples: Monte Oliveto. Liguori Chapel. Altar (xv century)
Naples: Monte Oliveto. Chapelle Liguori. Autel (xve siècle)

122. Naples: Santa Maria del Carmine (XII-XIII century)
Naples: Santa Maria del Carmine (XIIe-XIIIe siècle)

123. Naples: Santa Chiara (XIV-XVIII century)
Naples: Santa Chiara (XIVe-XVIIIe siècle)

124. Naples: Santa Chiara. Tomb of Robert the Wise (XIV century)
Naples: Santa Chiara. Tombeau de Robert le Sage (XIVe siècle)

125. Monte Cassino: Abbey (Founded in VIth century)
Mont-Cassin: L'Abbaye (Fondée au VIe siècle)

126. Monte Cassino: Ruins of the Abbey
Mont-Cassin: L'Abbaye en Ruines

127. Monte Cassino: Abbey: Entrance Courtyard (XVII century)
    Mont-Cassin: L'Abbaye: La Cour d'Entrée (XVIIe siècle)

128. Monte Cassino: Abbey: Sacristy of the Cathedral (XVII century)
    Mont-Cassin: L'Abbaye: Sacristie de la Cathédrale (XVIIe siècle)

129. Rome: San Lorenzo Outside-the-Walls (XIII-XVIII century)
Rome: Saint-Laurent Hors-les-Murs (XIIIe-XVIIIe siècle)

130. Rome: Ruins of San Lorenzo Outside-the-Walls
Rome: Saint-Laurent Hors-les-Murs en Ruines

131. Frascati: Villa Falconieri (XVI century)
    Frascati: Villa Falconieri (XVIe siècle)

132. Frascati: Villa Lancellotti (XVI century)
    Frascati: Villa Lancellotti (XVIe siècle)

133. Palestrina: Barberini Palace (xv century)
Palestrina: Palais Barberini (xve siècle)

134. Valmontone: Doria-Pamphili Palace (XVII century)
    Valmontone: Palais Doria-Pamphili (XVIIe siècle)

135. Tarquinia: Vitelleschi Palace (1439)
    Tarquinia: Palais Vitelleschi (1439)

136. Terni: San Francesco. Ceiling (XVI century)
Terni: San Francesco. Plafond (XVIe siècle)

37. Terni: San Francesco (XIII century)
Terni: San Francesco (XIIIe siècle)

38. Viterbo: San Sisto (IX-XII century)
Viterbe: San Sisto (IXe-XIIe siècle)

140. Viterbo: Santa Maria della Verità. Lorenzo da Viterbo: Marriage of the Virgin (XV century)
Viterbe: Santa Maria della Verità. Lorenzo da Viterbo: Mariage de la Vierge (XVe siècle)

141. Viterbo: Santa Maria della Verità. Lorenzo da Viterbo: Evangelists (xv century)
Viterbe: Santa Maria della Verità. Lorenzo da Viterbo: Evangélistes (xve siècle)

142. Viterbo: Fountain. Piazza della Rocca (1575)
     Viterbe: Fontaine. Piazza della Rocca (1575)

143. Viterbo: San Giovanni in Zoccoli (XI century)
     Viterbe: San Giovanni in Zoccoli (XIe siècle)

144. Siena: Osservanza Church (xv century)
Sienne: Eglise de l'Osservanza (xve siècle)

145. Siena: Osservanza Church. Andrea della Robbia: Coronation of the Virgin

Sienne: Eglise de l'Osservanza. Andrea della Robbia: Couronnement de la Vierge

146. San Gimignano: Collegiata. Barna da Siena: Crucifixion (xv century)
San Gimignano: Collegiata. Barna da Siena: Crucifiement (xve siècle)

147. San Gimignano: Collegiata. Barna da Siena: The Marriage at Cana
San Gimignano: Collegiata. Barna da Siena: Les Noces de Cana

148. Badia a Settimo: Columbaione Tower (XIV century)
Badia a Settimo: Tour Columbaione (XIVe siècle)

149. Florence: Acciaioli Palace (XVI century) and the Lungarno
Florence: Palais Acciaioli (XVIe siècle) et le Lungarno

151. Florence: Santa Trinità Bridge. Statue of Summer (XVI century)
    Florence: Pont Santa Trinità. Statue d'Eté (XVIe siècle)

150. Florence: Santa Trinità Bridge. Statue of Autumn (XVI century)
    Florence: Pont Santa Trinità. Statue d'Automne (XVIe siècle)

152. Florence: Santa Trinità Bridge (XVI century)
      Florence: Pont Santa Trinità (XVIe siècle)

153. Florence: Borgo San Jacopo
Florence: Borgo San Jacopo

154. Florence: Ruins of the Lungarno Acciaioli, View from Borgo San Jacopo
Florence: Ruines du Lungarno Acciaioli, Vue de Borgo San Jacopo

155. Impruneta: Collegiata. Chapel of the Madonna (xv century)
Impruneta: Collegiata. Chapelle de la Madone (xve siècle)

156. Impruneta: Collegiata. Chapel of the Madonna. Luca della Robbia: Bas Relief
Impruneta: Collegiata. Chapelle de la Madone. Luca della Robbia: Bas Relief

157. **Impruneta: Collegiata. Chapel of the Holy Cross. Luca della Robbia: Altar (xv century)**
Impruneta: Collegiata. Chapelle de la Sainte Croix. Luca della Robbia: Autel (xvᵉ siècle)

8. Impruneta: Collegiata. Luca della Robbia: Bas Relief (xv century)
   Impruneta: Collegiata. Luca della Robbia: Bas Relief (xve siècle)

159. Impruneta: Collegiata. Pietro Nelli and Tommaso del Mazza: Altarpiece (XIV century)
Impruneta: Collegiata. Pietro Nelli et Tommaso del Mazza: Retable (XIVe siècle)

60. Impruneta: Collegiata. Pietro Nelli and Tommaso del Mazza: Altarpiece (detail)
Impruneta: Collegiata. Pietro Nelli et Tommaso del Mazza: Retable (détail)

161. Impruneta: Collegiata. Pietro Nelli and Tommaso del Mazza: Altarpiece (detail)
Impruneta: Collegiata. Pietro Nelli et Tommaso del Mazza: Retable (détail)

162. Impruneta: Collegiata. Pietro Nelli and Tommaso del Mazza: Altarpiece (detail)
Impruneta: Collegiata. Pietro Nelli et Tommaso del Mazza: Retable (détail)

163. Empoli: Collegiata. Francesco Botticini: Annunciation (xv century)
Empoli: Collegiata. Francesco Botticini: Annonciation (xve siècle)

164. Prato: Tabernacle by Filippino Lippi (1498)
Prato: Tabernacle de Filippino Lippi (1498)

165. Pisa: Ponte del Mezzo (XVI century)
Pise: Ponte del Mezzo (XVIᵉ siècle)

166. Pisa: Medici Palace (XI-XIV century)
Pise: Palais Médicis (XIe-XIVe siècle)

167. Pisa: San Paolo a Ripa d'Arno (XI-XII century)
Pise: San Paolo a Ripa d'Arno (XIe-XIIe siècle)

168. Pisa: Camposanto. Benozzo Gozzoli: The Epiphany (xv century)
Pise: Camposanto. Benozzo Gozzoli: L'Epiphanie (xve siècle)

169. Pisa: Camposanto. Benozzo Gozzoli: Tower of Babel (detail)
Pise: Camposanto. Benozzo Gozzoli: Tour de Babel (détail)

170. Pisa: Camposanto. Benozzo Gozzoli: Tower of Babel (detail)
Pise: Camposanto. Benozzo Gozzoli: Tour de Babel (détail)

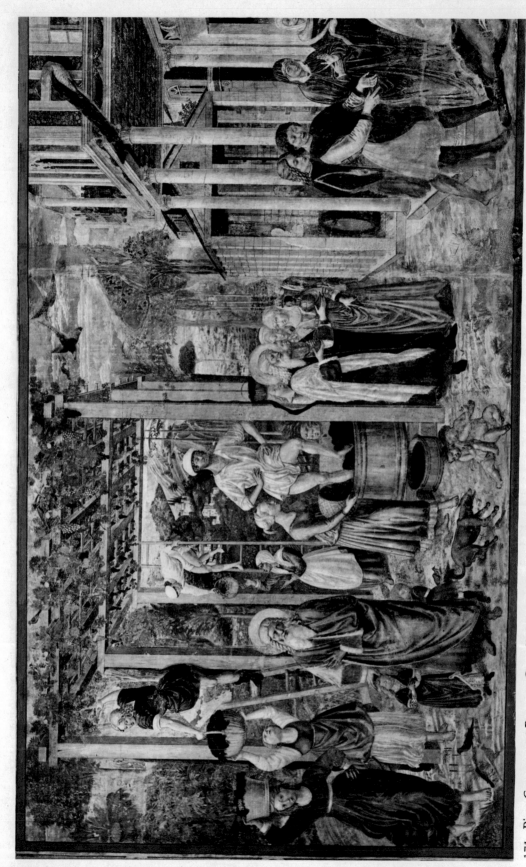

171. Pisa: Camposanto. Benozzo Gozzoli: Noah's Vintage and Drunkenness (detail)
Pise: Camposanto. Benozzo Gozzoli: Vendange et Ivresse de Noë (détail)

172. Pisa: Camposanto. Francesco Traini: Triumph of Death. Detail (XIV century)
Pise: Camposanto. Francesco Traini: Triomphe de la Mort. Détail (XIVe siècle)

173. Ancona: Santa Maria della Misericordia. Portal (XVI century)
Ancone: Santa Maria della Misericordia. Portail (XVIe siècle)

. Fano: Palazzo della Ragione
Fano: Palais della Ragione

175. Fano: San Paterniano. Campanile (XVI century)
Fano: San Paterniano. Campanile (XVIᵉ siècle)

176. Rimini: Temple of the Malatesta (XIV-XV century)

177. Rimini: Ruins of the Temple of the Malatesta
Rimini: Temple Malatesta en Ruines

178. Forli: San Biagio. Tomb of Barbara Manfredi (xv century)
Forli: San Biagio. Tombeau de Barbara Manfredi (xve siècle)

79. Forli: San Biagio. Melozzo da Forli and Palmezzano: Frescoes (XV century)
Forli: San Biagio. Melozzo da Forli et Palmezzano: Fresques (XVe siècle)

180. Forli: San Biagio. Melozzo da Forli and Palmezzano: Detail of Fresco (xv century)
Forli: San Biagio. Melozzo da Forli et Palmezzano: Détail de Fresque (xve siècle)

181. Forli: San Biagio. Melozzo da Forli and Palmezzano: Detail of Fresco (xv century)
Forli: San Biagio. Melozzo da Forli et Palmezzano: Détail de Fresque (xve siècle)

182. Bologna: Corpus Domini Church. Portal (xv century)
Bologne: Eglise Corpus Domini. Portail (xve siècle)

183. Bologna: San Francesco (XIII century)
    Bologne: San Francesco (XIIIe siècle)

184. Bologna: Archiginnasio. Anatomical Theatre. Ceiling (XVI century)
Bologne: Archiginnasio. Salle Anatomique. Plafond (XVIe siècle)

185. Bologna: Archiginnasio. Anatomical Theatre (XVI century)
Bologne: Archiginnasio. Salle Anatomique (XVIe siècle)

186. Parma: Farnèse Theatre (1617)
Parme: Théâtre Farnèse (1617)

187. Parma: Farnese Theatre (1617)
Parme: Théâtre Farnèse (1617)

188. Genoa: Negrone Palace (XVI century)
    Gênes: Palais Negrone (XVIe siècle)

9. Genoa: San Stefano (XII-XV century)
Gênes: San Stefano (XIIᵉ-XVᵉ siècle)

191. Genoa: Pallavicini Palace (XVII century)
Gênes: Palais Pallavicini (XVIIᵉ siècle)

192. Genoa: Sant' Annunziata del Vastato (XVII century)
    Gênes: Sant' Annunziata del Vastato (XVIIe siècle)

193. Genoa: Via Balbi
Gênes: Via Balbi

194. Turin: Palazzo del l'Università (XVIII century)
Turin: Palais de l'Université (XVIIIe siècle)

195. Turin: Palazzo Madama (XVIII century)
Turin: Palais Madama (XVIIIe siècle)

196. Milan: Ospedale Maggiore. Court (XV-XVII century)
Milan: L'Ospedale Maggiore. Cour (XVe-XVIIe siècle)

197. Milan: Marino Palace. Detail of the Court (XVI century)
Milan: Palais Marino. Détail de la Cour (XVIe siècle)

198. Milan: Santa Maria delle Grazie. Cloisters (xv century)
Milan: Santa Maria delle Grazie. Le Cloître (xve siècle)

199. Milan: Royal Palace. Hall of the Caryatides (XVIII century)
Milan: Palais Royal. Salle des Caryatides (XVIIIe siècle)

200. Milan: San Ambrogio. Sacristy. G. B. Tiepolo: Saint Bernard in Glory
Milan: San Ambrogio. Sacristie. G. B. Tiepolo: La Gloire de Saint Bernard

201. Milan: San Ambrogio. Bramante Portico (1492)
Milan: San Ambrogio. Portique de Bramante (1492)

202. Pavia: Bridge over the Ticino (XIV-XVI century)
Pavie: Pont sur le Tessin (XIVe-XVIe siècle)

203. Brescia: Salvadego Palace
Brescia: Palais Salvadego

204. Brescia: Santa Maria dei Miracoli (xv century)
Brescia: Santa Maria dei Miracoli (xve siècle)

205. Verona: Scaligero Bridge (XIV century)
Vérone: Pont Scaliger (XIVe siècle)

206. Verona: Ponte della Pietra (Roman Bridge)
Vérone: Ponte della Pietra (Pont Romain)

207. Vicenza: Piazza dei Signori and Basilica Palladiana (XVI century)
Vicence: Piazza dei Signori et Basilique Palladienne (XVIe siècle)

08. Vicenza: Monte di Pietà (XVI century)
Vicence: Le Mont de Piété (XVIe siècle)

210. Vicenza: Valmarana Palace (1566)
Vicence: Palais Valmarana (1566)

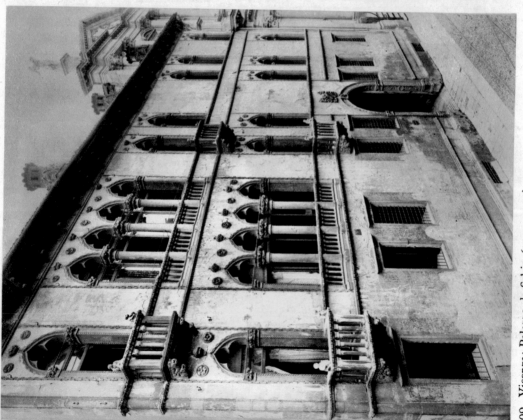

209. Vicenza: Palazzo da Schio (xv century)
Vicence: Palais da Schio (xve siècle)

212. Ravenna: Santa Maria in Porto fuori (XI-XIV century)
Ravenne: Santa Maria in Porto fuori (XIe-XIVe siècle)

211. Ravenna: Santa Maria in Porto fuori (XI-XIV century)
Ravenne: Santa Maria in Porto fuori (XIe-XIVe siècle)

213. Padua: Eremitani Church. Mantegna: Saint James being led to his Martyrdom (detail)
Padoue: L'Eglise des Eremitani. Mantegna: Saint Jacques conduit au martyre (détail)

214. Padua: Eremitani Church. Mantegna: Saint James being led to his Martyrdom
Padoue: L'Eglise des Eremitani. Mantegna: Saint Jacques conduit au Martyre

215. Padua: Eremitani Church. Mantegna: Death of Saint James
Padoue: L'Eglise des Eremitani. Mantegna: Mort de Saint Jacques

216. Padua: Eremitani Church. Mantegna: Baptism of Hermogenes
Padoue: L'Eglise des Eremitani. Mantegna: Baptême d'Hermogènes

217. Padua: Eremitani Church. Squarcione: Frescoes of Vaulting
Padoue: L'Eglise des Eremitani. Squarcione: Fresques de la Voûte

219. Pola: Duomo (VI century)
Pola: Le Dôme (VIe siècle)

218. Pola: Temple of Rome and Augustus (2–14 A.D.)
Pola: Temple de Rome et d'Auguste (2–14 A.D.)

220. Saint-Malo: Spire of Saint-Vincent (xv century) and Grande Rue
Saint-Malo: La Flèche de Saint-Vincent (xve siècle) et Grande Rue

221. Saint-Malo: General View
     Saint-Malo: Vue Générale

222. Saint-Malo: "Grande Porte" (xv century)
     Saint-Malo: La Grande Porte (xve siècle)

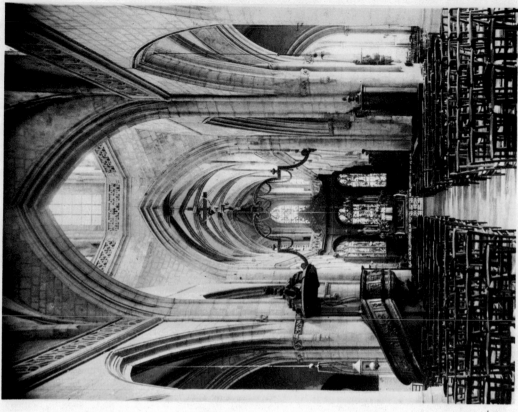

224. Valognes: Church. Choir and Apse (XIV century)
Valognes: Eglise. Chœur et Abside (XIVe siècle)

223. Valognes: Church (XIV century)
Valognes: Eglise (XIVe siècle)

226. Lessay: Abbey Church (xi century)
Lessay: Eglise de l'Abbaye (xie siècle)

225. Lessay: Abbey Church (xi century)
Lessay: Eglise de l'Abbaye (xie siècle)

227. Saint-Lô: Cathedral of Notre-Dame (XIII century)
Saint-Lô: Cathédrale Notre-Dame (XIIIe siècle)

28. Saint-Lô: Ruins of the Cathedral of Notre-Dame
Saint-Lô: Cathédrale Notre-Dame en Ruines

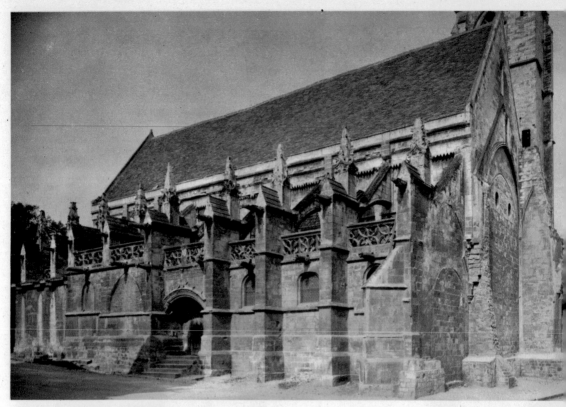

229. Caen: Church of Saint-Gilles (XI–XIII century)
Caen: Eglise Saint-Gilles (XIe–XIIIe siècle)

230. Caen: Church of Saint-Gilles (XI–XIII century)
Caen: Eglise Saint-Gilles (XIe–XIIIe siècle)

1. Caen: Escoville Mansion (1538)
   Caen: Hôtel d'Escoville (1538)

232. Caen: Church of Saint-Pierre (XIV century)
Caen: Eglise Saint-Pierre (XIVe siècle)

33. Caen: Ruins of Church of Saint-Pierre
Caen: Eglise Saint-Pierre en Ruines

234. Caen: City Hall (XVIII century)
Caen: Hôtel de Ville (XVIIIe siècle)

236. Colleville-sur-Mer: Church (XII century)
Colleville-sur-Mer: Eglise (XIIᵉ siècle)

235. Caen: Castle. Portal (XI century)
Caen: Château. Portail (XIᵉ siècle)

237. Caen: "Than" Mansion (XVI century)
    Caen: Hôtel de Than (XVIᵉ siècle)

238. Saint-Pierre-sur-Dives: Market (XIII century)
    Saint-Pierre-sur-Dives: Halles (XIIIᵉ siècle)

239. Billy: Church (XIII century)
Billy: Eglise (XIIIe siècle)

240. Carrouges: Gate-House (XVII century)
Carrouges: Châtelet (XVIIe siècle)

241. Norrey: Church (XIII century)
Norrey: Eglise (XIIIe siècle)

242. Saint-Sylvain: Church (XI century)
Saint-Sylvain: Eglise (XIe siècle)

243. Courseulles-sur-Mer: Chateau (XVII century)
Courseulles-sur-Mer: Château (XVIIe siècle)

244. Falaise: Church of Saint-Gervais (XI–XIII century)
Falaise: Eglise Saint-Gervais (XIe–XIIIe siècle)

245. Falaise: Church of the Trinity (XIII–XV century)
Falaise: Eglise de la Trinité (XIIIe–XVe siècle)

246. Pont-l'Evêque: Brilly Mansion (XVIII century)
Pont-l'Evêque: Hôtel de Brilly (XVIIIe siècle)

7. Pont-l'Evêque: The "Island" Manor
Pont-l'Evêque: Manoir de l'Ile

248. Lisieux: The "Salamander" House (XVI century)
Lisieux: Maison de la Salamandre (XVIe siècle)

250. Lisieux: Rue aux Fèves (XVI century)
Lisieux: Rue aux Fèves (XVIᵉ siècle)

249. Lisieux: The "Salamander" House. Doorway (XVI century)
Lisieux: Maison de la Salamandre. Portail (XVIᵉ siècle)

251. Lisieux: Church of Saint-Jacques (xv century)
Lisieux: Eglise Saint-Jacques (xve siècle)

2. Argentan: Church of Saint-Germain (XV–XVII century)
   Argentan: Eglise Saint-Germain (XVe–XVIIe siècle)

3. Argentan: Church of Saint-Germain in Ruins
   Argentan: Eglise Saint-Germain en Ruines

254. Caudebec-en-Caux: House of the Templars (XIII century)
Caudebec-en-Caux: Maison des Templiers (XIIIe siècle)

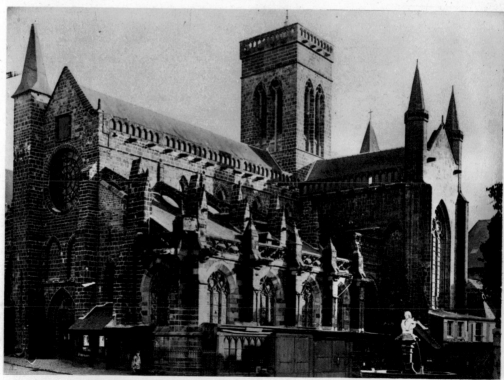

255. Vire: Church of Notre-Dame (XIII–XV century)
Vire: Eglise Notre-Dame (XIIIe–XVe siècle)

256. Rouen: General View
Rouen: Vue Générale

257. Rouen: Cathedral. South Aisle (XIII century)
Rouen: La Cathédrale. Bas Côté Sud (XIIIe siècle)

258. Rouen: Cathedral. North Transept Rose (1481)
Rouen: La Cathédrale. La Rosace du Transept Nord (1481)

259. Rouen: Law-Courts (XVI century)
    Rouen: Palais de Justice (XVIe siècle)

260. Rouen: Law-Courts. Court-Room (XVI century)
Rouen: Palais de Justice. Salle des Assises (XVIe siècle)

261. Rouen: Bourgtheroulde Mansion (xv century)
Rouen: Hôtel du Bourgtheroulde (xve siècle)

262. Rouen: House of Diane de Poitiers (XVI century)
Rouen: Maison de Diane de Poitiers (XVIe siècle)

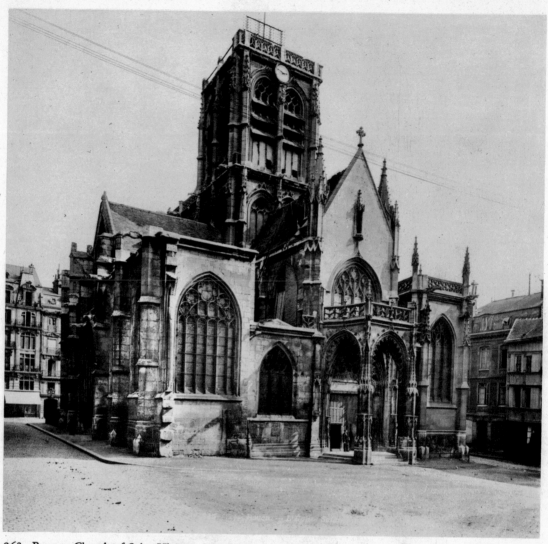

263. Rouen: Church of Saint-Vincent (xv century)
Rouen: Eglise Saint-Vincent (xve siècle)

264. Abbeville: Church of Saint-Vulfran. Choir (XV century)
Abbeville: Eglise Saint-Vulfran. Le Chœur (XVe siècle)

265. Amiens: The "Sagittaire" Mansion (XVI century)
      Amiens: Maison du Sagittaire (XVIe siècle)

266. Amiens: Church of Saint-Germain. Portal (xv century)
Amiens: Eglise Saint-Germain. Portail (xve siècle)

267. Amiens: Bailiff's Courthouse (XVI century)
Amiens: Le Bailliage (XVIe siècle)

269. Calais: City Hall (XVI–XVIII century)
Calais: Hôtel de Ville (XVIᵉ–XVIIIᵉ siècle)

268. Calais: Porte de Guise
Calais: Porte de Guise

270. Beauvais: General View. Houses around the Cathedral
Beauvais: Vue Générale. Maisons autour de la Cathédrale

271. Beauvais: Destroyed Area around the Cathedral
Beauvais: Quartier détruit autour de la Cathédrale

272. Cassel: Town Hall (XVI–XVII century)
Cassel: Hôtel de Ville (XVIᵉ–XVIIᵉ siècle)

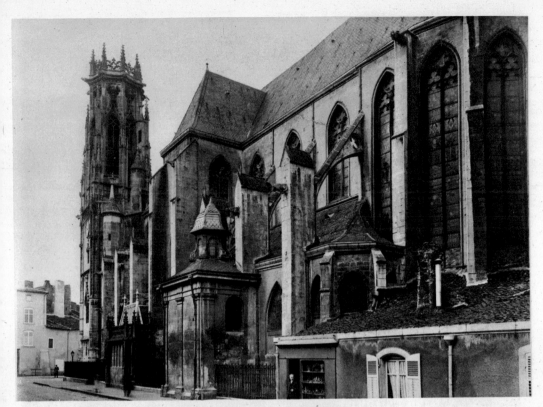

273. Pont-à-Mousson: Saint Martin's Church (XIII–XIV century)
Pont-à-Mousson: Eglise Saint-Martin (XIIIe–XIVe siècle)

274. Toul: City Hall (XVIII century)
Toul: Hôtel de Ville (XVIIIe siècle)

275. Toul: Cathedral of Saint-Etienne (XIII century)
Toul: Cathédrale Saint-Etienne (XIIIe siècle)

276. Toul: Cathedral of Saint-Etienne (XIII century)
Toul: Cathédrale Saint-Etienne (XIIIe siècle)

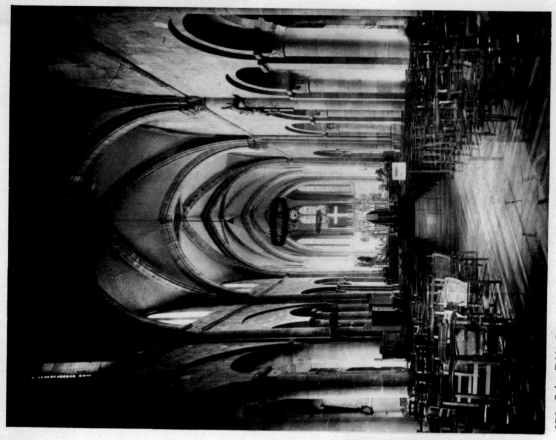

278. Saint-Dié: Cathedral
Saint-Dié: La Cathédrale

277. Saint-Dié: Cathedral
Saint-Dié: La Cathédrale

280. Rethel: Church of Saint-Nicholas (XIII century)
Rethel: Église Saint-Nicolas (XIIIe siècle)

279. Strasbourg: Church of Saint-Etienne
Strasbourg: Église Saint-Etienne

281. Châteaudun: Church of the "Madeleine" (XII century)
Châteaudun: Eglise de la Madeleine (XIIe siècle)

282. Chartres: "Porte Guillaume" (XIV century)
    Chartres: Porte Guillaume (XIVe siècle)

283. Verneuil: Church of the 'Madeleine.' Top of Spire (XVI century)
Verneuil: Eglise de la Madeleine. Sommet de la Tour (XVIe siècle)

284. Gisors: Church of Saint-Gervais and Saint-Protais. West Façade (XVI century)
Gisors: Eglise de Saint-Gervais et Saint-Protais. Façade Occidentale (XVIᵉ siècle)

285. Vendôme: Town Hall (XIV century)
Vendôme: Hôtel de Ville (XIVe siècle)

286. Nevers: Cathedral of Saint-Cyr (XI–XVI century)
Nevers: Cathédrale Saint-Cyr (XIe–XVIe siècle)

287. Orleans: House of Agnes Sorel (XVI century)
Orléans: Maison d'Agnès Sorel (XVIe siècle)

88. Orleans: Turret (xv century)
Orléans: Tourelle (xve siècle)

289. Saint-Aignan: Chateau (XVI century)
Saint-Aignan: Château (XVIᵉ siècle)

290. Saint-Aignan: Church (XI–XII century)
Saint-Aignan: Eglise (XIe–XIIe siècle)

291. Tours: Mansion of the White Cross
Tours: Hôtel de la Croix-Blanche

92. Tours: Gouin Mansion (xv century)
    Tours: Hôtel Gouin (xve siècle)

293. Pernes-Les-Fontaines: Gateway of Notre-Dame (1548)

Pernes-Les-Fontaines: Porte Notre-Dame (1548)

294. Marseilles: Old Waterfront
Marseille: Vieux Port

295. Aachen: City Hall (XIV century)
Aix-la-Chapelle: Hôtel de Ville (XIVe siècle)

296. Aachen: Minster (VIII–XV century)
     Aix-la-Chapelle: La Cathédrale (VIIIe–XVe siècle)

297. Brühl: Schloss Brühl (XVIII century)
     Brühl: Château Brühl (XVIIIe siècle)

298. Neuss: Church of Saint Quirinus. Choir (XIII century)
Neuss: Eglise Saint-Quirin. Chœur (XIIIe siècle)

299. Neuss: Church of Saint Quirinus. East Tower (XIII–XVIII century)
Neuss: Eglise Saint-Quirin. Tour occidentale (XIIIe–XVIIIe siècle)

300. Cologne: Church of Saint Gereon (XIII century)
Cologne: Eglise Saint-Géréon (XIIIe siècle)

301. Cologne: Church of Saint Gereon. Nave (XI–XIII century)
Cologne: Eglise Saint-Géréon. Nef (XIe–XIIIe siècle)

302. Cologne: St. Maria im Capitol (XI century)
Cologne: St. Maria im Capitol (XIe siècle)

303. Cologne: Church of Saint Andrew (XIII–XV century)
Cologne: Eglise Saint-André (XIIIᵉ–XVᵉ siècle)

304. Cologne: Gürzenich (Festival Hall, XV century)
Cologne: Gürzenich (Salle des Fêtes, XVe siècle)

Cologne: Gross St. Martin (XII–XIII century)
Cologne: Gross St. Martin (XIIe–XIIIe siècle)

306. Cologne: City Hall. Porch (XVI century)
Cologne: Hôtel de Ville. Portique (XVIe siècle)

. Cologne: City Hall (XIV–XVI century)
Cologne: Hôtel de Ville (XIVe–XVIe siècle)

309. Cologne: Church of Saint Ursula (XI–XV century)
Cologne: Eglise Sainte-Ursule (XIe–XVe siècle)

308. Cologne: City Hall. Hansa Saal (XIV century)
Cologne: Hôtel de Ville. Salle Hanséatique (XIVe siècle)

311. Paderborn: Cathedral (xɪ–xv century)
Paderborn: La Cathédrale (xɪɪe–xve siècle)

310. Paderborn: City Hall (xvɪɪ century)
Paderborn: Hôtel de Ville (xvɪɪe siècle)

312. Münster: Town Hall (XIV century)
Munster: Hôtel de Ville (XIVe siècle)

313. Münster: Church of Saint Ludger (XIII–XIV century)
Munster: Eglise Saint-Ludger (XIIIe–XIVe siècle)

315. Münster: City Wine House (XVII century)
Munster: Halle aux Vins (XVIIᵉ siècle)

314. Münster: Cathedral (XIII century)
Munster: La Cathédrale (XIIIᵉ siècle)

316. Minden: Cathedral. Choir (XIII century)
Minden: La Cathédrale. Chœur (XIIIe siècle)

317. Xanten: Collegiate Church of St. Victor (XIII–XVI century)
Xanten: Eglise Collégiale de Saint-Victor (XIIIᵉ–XVIᵉ siècle)

318. Osnabrück: Cathedral of Saint Peter and Saint Paul (XII–XIII century)
Osnabruck: Cathédrale de Saint-Pierre et Saint-Paul (XIIe–XIIIe siècle)

319. Mainz: Market Place
Mayence: Place du Marché

321. Mainz: Electoral Palace (XVII century)
Mayence: Palais de l'Electeur (XVIIe siècle)

320. Mainz: Saint Peter's Church (XVIII century)
Mayence: Eglise Saint-Pierre (XVIIIe siècle)

322. Coblenz: Church of St. Castor (x–xiii century)
Coblence: Eglise Saint-Castor (xe–xiiie siècle)

323. Trier: Market Place with "Rotes Haus" (xv century)
     Trèves: Place du Marché et "Rotes Haus" (xve siècle)

324. Trier: Abbey of Saint Matthew (xi–xiii century)
     Trèves: Abbaye Saint-Matthieu (xie–xiiie siècle)

325. Trier: Church of Our Lady. Portal (XIII century)
Trèves: Eglise Notre-Dame. Portail (XIIIe siècle)

6. Trier: Church of Our Lady (XIII century)
Trèves: Eglise Notre-Dame (XIIIe siècle)

327. Trier: Kesselstadt Palace (xviii century)
Trèves: Palais Kesselstadt (xviiie siècle)

328. Cassel: Orangerie Schloss (xviii century)
Cassel: Orangerie (xviiie siècle)

9. Giessen: The Old Schloss (xv–xvi century)
   Giessen: Le Vieux Château (xve–xvie siècle)

0. Darmstadt: Grand-Ducal Palace (xvi–xviii century)
   Darmstadt: Palais du Grand Duc (xvie–xviiie siècle)

331. Darmstadt: Market Place
Darmstadt: Place du Marché

32. Darmstadt: Ruins of Market Place
Darmstadt: Place du Marché en ruines

333. Worms: Saint Paul's Church (XIII century)
Worms: Eglise Saint-Paul (XIIIe siècle)

334. Frankfurt: The Römer (City Hall, xv–xvi century)
Francfort: Le Römer (Hôtel de Ville, xvᵉ–xvɪᵉ siècle)

335. Frankfurt: Domplatz
Francfort: Domplatz

337. Frankfurt: Alter Markt
Francfort: Alter Markt

336. Frankfurt: House "Zur Goldenen Waage" (1624)
Francfort: La Maison "Zur Goldenen Waage" (1624)

339. Frankfurt: City Hall. Staircase (XVI century)
Francfort: Hôtel de Ville. Escalier (XVIe siècle)

338. Frankfurt: Church of Our Lady. South Portal (XV century)
Francfort: Eglise Notre-Dame. Portail Sud (XVe siècle)

340. Aschaffenburg: Schloss (XVII century)
Aschaffenburg: Le Château (XVIIe siècle)

341. Aschaffenburg: Schloss (XVII century)
  Aschaffenburg: Le Château (XVIIe siècle)

342: Mannheim: Schloss (XVIII century)
  Mannheim: Le Château (XVIIIe siècle)

343. Bruchsal: Schloss (XVIII century)
Bruchsal: Le Château (XVIIIe siècle)

344. Bruchsal: Schloss. "Fürstensaal" (XVIII century)
Bruchsal: Le Château. "Fürstensaal" (XVIIIe siècle)

45. Karlsruhe: Schloss (XVIII century)
    Karlsruhe: Le Château (XVIIIe siècle)

346. Karlsruhe: Schloss Gottesaue (XVI century)
     Karlsruhe: Château Gottesaue (XVIe siècle)

347. Stuttgart: Stiftskirche (XIV–XV century)
Stuttgart: Eglise Conventuelle (XIVe–XVe siècle)

348. Stuttgart: Old Palace. Courtyard (XVI century)
Stuttgart: Le Vieux Palais. Cour (XVIᴇ siècle)

349. Stuttgart: Old Palace (XVI century)
Stuttgart: Le Vieux Palais (XVIe siècle)

350. Stuttgart: New Palace (XVIII century)
      Stuttgart: Le Nouveau Palais (XVIIIᵉ siècle)

351. Ulm: Town Hall (XIV century)
    Ulm: Hôtel de Ville (XIVe siècle)

352. Ulm: City Wall and Old Houses adjoining Cathedral
    Ulm: Remparts de la Ville et Vieilles Maisons près de la Cathédrale

353. Ulm: Schwörhaus (XVII century)
Ulm: Schwörhaus (XVIIe siècle)

354. Ulm: Section adjoining Cathedral
Ulm: Quartier près de la Cathédrale

55. Ulm: Ruined Section
Ulm: Quartier en ruines

356. Freiburg: Basler Hof (XVI century)
Fribourg: Basler Hof (XVIe siècle)

358. Heilbronn: Saint Kilian's Church in Ruins
Heilbronn: Eglise Saint-Kilian en ruines

357. Heilbronn: Saint Kilian's Church (XV–XVI century)
Heilbronn: Eglise Saint-Kilian (XVe–XVIe siècle)

359. Heilbronn: Market Place and Saint Kilian's Church
Heilbronn: Place du Marché et Eglise Saint-Kilian

360. Heilbronn: Town Hall (XIV–XVI century)
Heilbronn: Hôtel de Ville (XIVe–XVIe siècle)

361. Würzburg: Residenz. Interior (XVIII century)
Wurtzbourg: Residenz. Intérieur (XVIIIe siècle)

362. Würzburg: Residenz. Mirror Room (detail)
Wurtzbourg: Residenz. Salle des Miroirs (détail)

364. Würzburg: Marienkapelle (XIV–XV century)
Wurtzbourg: Marienkapelle (XIVe–XVe siècle)

363. Würzburg: Marienkapelle and Haus zum Falken
Wurtzbourg: Marienkapelle et Haus zum Falken

366. Würzburg: Stift Haug (XVII century)
Wurzbourg: Stift Haug (XVIIe siècle)

365. Würzburg: Old University (XVI century)
Wurzbourg: Vieille Université (XVIe siècle)

368. Bamberg: Town Hall (XVIII century)
Bamberg: Hôtel de Ville (XVIIIe siècle)

367. Würzburg: Neumünster Church. Façade (XVIII century)
Wurtzbourg: Eglise Neumünster. Façade (XVIIIe siècle)

369. Rothenburg: Weisser Turm (XIII century)
Rothenbourg: Weisser Turm (XIIIe siècle)

370. Rothenburg: General View
Rothenbourg: Vue Générale

371. Rothenburg: Ruined Section
Rothenbourg: Quartier en ruines

372. Nuremberg: General View
Nuremberg: Vue Générale

373. Nuremberg: Ruins
Nuremberg: Ruines

374. Nuremberg: Houses on the Pegnitz
Nuremberg: Maisons sur le Pegnitz

375. Nuremberg: Peller House (1605)
Nuremberg: Hôtel Peller (1605)

376. Nuremberg: Frauenkirche (XIV century)
Nuremberg: Frauenkirche (XIVe siècle)

377. Nuremberg: Market Place
Nuremberg: Place du Marché

378. Nuremberg: Fleisch-Brücke (XVI century)
Nuremberg: Fleisch-Brücke (XVIe siècle)

379. Nuremberg: Holy Ghost Hospital. Courtyard (XV–XVI century)
Nuremberg: Hôpital du Saint-Esprit. Cour (XVe–XVIe siècle)

380. Munich: Marienplatz, with old Town Hall (xv century)
Munich: Marienplatz et vieil Hôtel de Ville (xve siècle)

381. Munich: Frauenkirche (xv century)
    Munich: Frauenkirche (xve siècle)

382. Munich: Residenz. The Antiquarium (XVI century)
Munich: Residenz. L'Antiquarium (XVIe siècle)

384. Munich: Preysing Palace (XVIII century)
Munich: Palais Preysing (XVIIIe siècle)

383. Munich: Residenz. Courtyard (XVII century)
Munich: Residenz. Cour (XVIIe siècle)

385. Munich: Church of the Theatines (XVII–XVIII century)
Munich: Eglise des Théatins (XVIIe-XVIIIe siècle)

386B. Munich: Saint Anne's Church (XVIII century)
Munich: Eglise Sainte-Anne (XVIIIe siècle)

386A. Munich: Saint Anne's Church (XVIII century)
Munich: Eglise Sainte-Anne (XVIIIe siècle)

387. Munich: Saint Michael's Church (XVI century)
    Munich: Eglise Saint-Michel (XVIe siècle)

388. Augsburg: Town Hall: Golden Hall (1623)
    Augsbourg: Hôtel de Ville: Salle Dorée (1623)

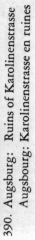

390. Augsburg: Ruins of Karolinenstrasse
Augsbourg: Karolinenstrasse en ruines

389. Augsburg: Karolinenstrasse
Augsbourg: Karolinenstrasse

391. Augsburg: Fugger House (1512)
Augsbourg: Hôtel Fugger (1512)

393. Esslingen: Town Hall. (XV–XVI century)
Esslingen: Hôtel de Ville. (XVe–XVIe siècle)

392. Esslingen: Town Hall. Facade (XV–XVI century)
Esslingen: Hôtel de Ville. Façade (XVe–XVIe siècle)

394. Hildesheim: Kaiserhaus (1586)
Hildesheim: Kaiserhaus (1586)

395. Hildesheim: Knochenhauer-Amtshaus (1529)
Hildesheim: Knochenhauer-Amtshaus (1529)

96. Hildesheim: Ruins of Knochenhauer-Amtshaus
   Hildesheim: Knochenhauer-Amtshaus en ruines

397. Hildesheim: Saint Michael's Church (XI–XII century)
Hildesheim: Eglise Saint-Michel (XIe–XIIe siècle)

398. Hildesheim: Saint Andrew's Church (XII–XV century)
Hildesheim: Eglise Saint-André (XIIe–XVe siècle)

399. Brunswick: Old Town Hall (XIV–XV century)
Brunswick: Vieil Hôtel de Ville (XIVe–XVe siécle)

400. Brunswick: Old House (xv century)
Brunswick: Vieille Maison (xve siècle)

401. Dresden: Passage from Hofkirche to Schloss (XVIII century)
    Dresde: Passage de l'Hofkirche au Palais (XVIIIe siècle)

402. Dresden: Hofkirche (XVIII century)
Dresde: Hofkirche (XVIIIe siècle)

403. Dresden: Zwinger (XVIII century)
Dresde: Zwinger (XVIIIe siècle)

404. Dresden: Zwinger (XVIII century)
    Dresde: Zwinger (XVIIIe siècle)

406. Dresden: Ruins of the Frauenkirche
Dresde: Frauenkirche en ruines

405. Dresden: Frauenkirche (XVIII century)
Dresde: Frauenkirche (XVIIIe siècle)

404. Dresden: Zwinger (XVIII century)
Dresde: Zwinger (XVIIIe siècle)

406. Dresden: Ruins of the Frauenkirche
Dresde: Frauenkirche en ruines

405. Dresden: Frauenkirche (XVIII century)
Dresde: Frauenkirche (XVIIIe siècle)

407. Lübeck: Town Hall Square and the Marienkirche (xiii–xv century)
Lubeck: Place de l'Hôtel de Ville et Marienkirche (xiiie–xve siècle)

408. Lübeck: Marienkirche (XIV century)
Lubeck: Marienkirche (XIVe siècle)

409. Lübeck: Town Hall (XIII–XV century)
Lubeck: Hôtel de Ville (XIIIe–XVe siècle)

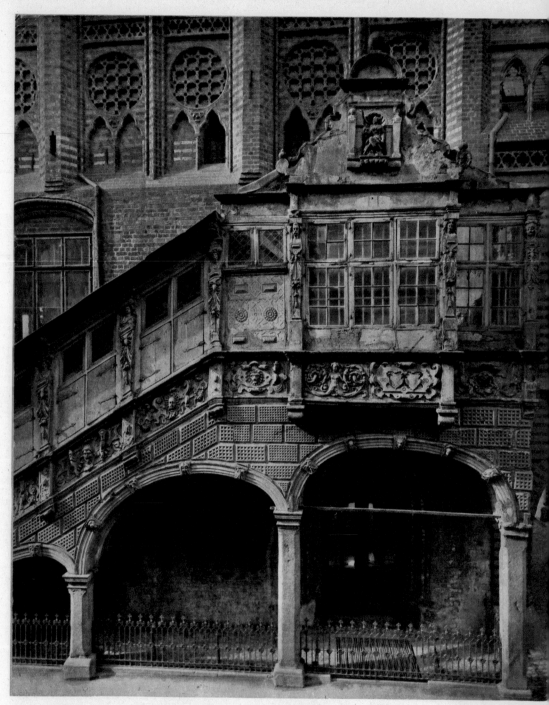

410. Lübeck: Town Hall. Staircase (1594)
　　Lubeck: Hôtel de Ville. Escalier (1594)

411. Lübeck: The Salt Houses (XIV century)
Lubeck: Entrepôts de Sel (XIVe siècle)

412. Emden: Town Hall (1576)
Emden: Hôtel de Ville (1576)

413. Hamburg: Canal off the Binnenhafen
Hambourg: Canal dans le Binnenhafen

414. Königsberg: Schloss (XIII-XVI century)
    Kœnigsberg: Château (XIIIe–XVIe siècle)

415. Berlin: Charlottenburg Schloss (XVII–XVIII century)
Berlin: Palais de Charlottenburg (XVIIᵉ–XVIIIᵉ siècle)

416. Berlin: Französische Kirche (XVIII century)
Berlin: L'Eglise Française (XVIIIe siècle)

417. Berlin: Ruins of the Französische Kirche
Berlin: L'Eglise Française en ruines

418. Berlin: The Royal Palace (XVIII century)
Berlin: Le Palais Royal (XVIIIe siècle)

419. Berlin: Schloss Monbijou (1706)
Berlin: Palais Monbijou (1706)

420. Vienna: Schloss Belvedere (XVIII century)
Vienne: Palais Belvédère (XVIIIe siècle)

421. Vienna: Stefansdom and "Innere Stadt"
Vienne: Stefansdom et "Innere Stadt"

422. Vienna: Stefansdom. Vaulting (xv century)
Vienne: Stefansdom. Voûtes (xve siècle)

423. Vienna: Kinsky Palace (xVIII century)
Vienne: Palais Kinsky (xVIIIe siècle)

424. Budapest: Royal Palace (XVIII century)
Budapest: Le Palais Royal (XVIIIe siècle)

425. Budapest: Ruins of the Royal Palace and Széchenyi Bridge
Budapest: Le Palais Royal et Pont Széchenyi en ruines

426. Budapest: Royal Palace. Façade (XVIII century)
Budapest: Le Palais Royal. Façade (XVIIIe siècle)

427. Budapest: Royal Palace. Interior (XVIII century)
Budapest: Le Palais Royal. Intérieur (XVIIIe siècle)